The Meaning of
Crisis

The Meaning of Crisis

A Theoretical Introduction

JAMES O'CONNOR

Basil Blackwell

Pfeiffer Library
Pfeiffer College
Misenheimer, N. C. 28109

125814

Copyright © James O'Connor 1987

First published 1987

Basil Blackwell Ltd
108 Cowley Road, Oxford, OX4 1JF, UK

Basil Blackwell Inc.
432 Park Avenue South, Suite 1503
New York, NY 10016, USA

All rights reserved. Except for the quotation of short passages for the purposes of criticism and review, no part of this publication may be reproduced, stored in a retrieval system, or transmitted, in any form or by any means, electronic, mechanical, photocopying, recording or otherwise, without the prior permission of the publisher.

Except in the United States of America, this book is sold subject to the condition that it shall not, by way of trade or otherwise, be lent, re-sold, hired out, or otherwise circulated without the publisher's prior consent in any form of binding or cover other than that in which it is published and without a similar condition including this condition being imposed on the subsequent purchaser.

British Library Cataloguing in Publication Data

O'Connor, James
    1. Depressions   2. Marxist economics
    3. Capitalism
    I. Title
    338.5'4 HB3722

    ISBN 0-631-13821-8
    ISBN 0-631-13819-6 Pbk

Library of Congress Cataloging in Publication Data

O'Connor, James (James R.)
    The meaning of crisis.

    Includes index.
    1. Depressions. 2. Business cycles.
    3. Marxian economics. I. Title.
    HB3714.024 1987   338.5'4   86–26399
    ISBN 0-631-13821-8
    ISBN 0-631-13819-6 (pbk.)

Typeset in 11 on 13 pt Sabon
by Alan Sutton Publishing Limited, Gloucester
Printed in Great Britain by Billing and Sons Ltd, Worcester

Contents

Acknowledgements

I wish to thank the following friends and co-workers for their useful comments on various draft chapters of this work: Robert Alford, Saul Landau, Robert Marotto, Dale Tomich, and Dwayne Ward.

Preface

Introduction

This book is a critical survey of the main currents of modern economic, social, political, and personality crisis theory. It has two principal goals. The first is to introduce students who desire a handy catalogue of the subject to the most important Marxist and neo- and post-Marxist explanations of modern crisis trends and tendencies. There are three self-imposed limits on this survey. One is that it is not exhaustive, nor could it be, given its length. This study is rather an outline highlighting some of the main lines of thinking of political economists, sociologists, political scientists, and others who have addressed various aspects of the contemporary world capitalist crisis. Another limit is that the account of economic crisis theory is not intended to be technically rigorous in terms of the standards of professional journals. In order to make economics accessible to the non-professional and guard against a merely formal approach to the subject, I have presented the theory in a literary rather than a mathematical mode. The final limit is that the subject of "crisis" as an ideology of social control, or ideology of economic austerity, is more or less ignored. The reason is that a discussion of this subject presupposes a full account of the "symbolic uses of politics" in the capitalist public sphere, which is beyond the scope of this work.

The second goal of this book is to expound a critical "theory of crisis theories." There are four kinds of explanations of various aspects of the modern crisis put forward by bourgeois

1

economists, neo-orthodox Marxists, and neo- and post-Marxist
theorists.[1] These may be conveniently called market theory,
value theory, social theory, and social-psychological theory,
respectively. The subject of the market theory of crisis is system
disintegration of capitalist economy at the level of exchange or
market relationships. The subject of neo-orthodox Marxist
crisis theory is capitalist-system disintegration at the level of the
production and circulation of capital and capital accumulation.
The subject of social theory is capitalist social disintegration, and
that of social-psychological theory is personality disintegration.
These approaches to crisis theory are based on four progressively less objectified and formal levels of abstraction from the
palpable reality of capitalist daily life. It should be stressed that
none of these approaches to the modern crisis of capitalism is
"more correct" than any of the others. Rather, each is a
successively more concrete, less deterministic, and more "historically interior" interpretation than the one immediately
preceding it. Each is an increasingly less partial and more
substantive view of "reality," which progressively subsumes (or
"sublates") the views antecedent to it.[2]

   This second aim has practical as well as theoretical implications. Its theoretical significance (however limited, given the

---

[1] "Bourgeois economists" are those working within the mainstream of
neo-classical, Keynesian, or post-Keynesian thought. "Neo-orthodox Marxists" are those (such as Ernest Mandel) whose work remains more or less
within the parameters of Marx's own political economic theory. "Neo-
Marxist theorists" (such as Claus Offe and the present writer) work within a
deeply reformed Marxist paradigm and their publications contain revisions of
orthodox or classical Marxism which "neo-orthodox Marxists" generally find
unacceptable. "Post-Marxist" theories (such as that presented in the last
chapter of this book) refer to all attempts to develop a radical and critical
social psychological approach to the psychopathology of everyday capitalist
life.

[2] "As an ontological category, the 'subject' is the power of an entity to 'be
itself in its otherness.'. . . Only such a mode of existence can incorporate the
negative into the positive. Negative and positive cease to be opposed to each
other when the driving power of the subject makes negativity a part of the
subject's own unity. Hegel says that the subject 'mediates' . . . and 'sublates'
. . . the negativity. In the process the object does not dissolve into its various
qualitative or quantitative determinations, but is substantially held together
throughout its relations with other objects": Herbert Marcuse, *Reason and
Revolution: Hegel and the Rise of Social Theory* (New York, 1954), 69.

suggestive rather than exhaustive treatment of the subject) is to provide a critique of economic determinism and to demonstrate the explanatory power of neo- and post-Marxist social and social-psychological theory in the realm of material life. Its practical importance is meant to be political, not only in the "public sphere" of bourgeois party politics, community and rank-and-file movements, and new social movements, but also in the politics of family and personal life where there is more than ever a need for theoretical orientation and guidance. More specifically, the practical importance of this work is to show that "crisis" is not and cannot be merely an "objective" historical process (such as, for example, the turning point in an illness over which the victim has no control). "Crisis" is also a "subjective" historical process – a time when it is not possible to take for granted "normal" economic, social, and other relationships; a time for decision; and a time when what individuals actually do counts for something. This is congruent with the classical Greek meaning of crisis as the moment for deciding between uncertain or arguable evaluations of a disease or illness. In short, this work tries to open up crisis theory to more interpretive and less deterministic approaches, while attempting to avoid simple subjectivism or voluntarism.

Market Competition and Market Theory

The most objectified and formal level of capitalist society is the totality of exchange relationships which is conventionally called the "market." Exchange or market relationships are the process whereby property rights in labor power, raw materials, machinery, buildings, land, consumer goods, and credit are exchanged against one another through the medium of money, the "universal equivalent." In the capitalist market, real individuals are "bearers of commodities" and "commodity guardians" (to use Marx's expression) – mere personifications of exchange relationships themselves. Hence real individuals objectify themselves and others in the sense that they "abstract from" their own and others' identities as workers, lovers, friends, women or men, members of ethnic groups, and so on, as well as their own irreducibly singular human natures, or what Walt Whitman called the "me myself."

The most abstract and also the most superficial crisis theory is bourgeois market theory, which is an account of disjunctures or breakdowns in the transfer of property rights between capitalist enterprises and individuals. These disjunctures or breakdowns appear to be the cause as well as the consequence of economic crisis, since exchange relationships appear to be the central reality of capitalist life. This is so because they are the hidden way in which labor becomes social labor, or the basic social activity through which capital "makes itself public" or reveals itself. This may be illustrated by the fact that data about commodity prices, stock prices, interest rates, sales volumes, and other market information inundate the popular consciousness; that civil lawyers and judges do little else than try to ensure equitable and secure transfers of rights to property; that politicians promise little more than to support policies which will enhance the market value of their constituents' property; that the most common questions heard in developed capitalist society are "How much does it cost?" and "How much money is there in it?"

Market theorists abstract from what is commonly called "work" (excepting the issue of physical productivity per worker) or what Marxists call the imposition and exploitation of labor within specifically capitalist relations of production. This abstraction is "natural" because the capitalist labor process is a peculiar form of private property, a kind of "social secret" which the capitalist monopoly of private property in the means of production conceals from public view. The labor process is "known" therefore only to the degree that labor organizers, investigative journalists, sociologists of work, and others critically expose it to public scrutiny. Furthermore, market theory abstracts from social, cultural, and ideological relationships, not to speak of the real-life experiences of real human beings within and outside of the labor process.

Market theory is the foundation of the bourgeois world-view which holds that modern crisis trends such as state deficits, inflation, unemployment, Third World debt, and so on are the result of market disintegration and/or inadequate monetary incentives and penalties and/or (in macro-economic theory) disparities between physical production capacity and effective demand for commodities, excessively high interest rates, and so on (chapter 1). Neo-liberal bourgeois economists, in particular, regard market mechanisms as autonomous forces which tend toward stability and/or stable economic growth as a result of the free workings of "competition" and the "price mechanism." However, stable equilibria or growing productivity and growth may be disrupted or distorted by "excessive" government, labor union, or other "monopolistic" interference with free competition, or by the wrong kind of government intervention. A well-known example is the neo-liberal view that the current problems of capitalism are in large part the result of excessive government regulation, public deficits, and borrowing, which raise interest rates and hence discourage investment spending.[3]

Production Relations and Value Theory

Chapter 1 outlines the surface manifestations of the modern crisis of capitalist economy and sketches some of the lines of analysis of the crisis put forward by bourgeois economists. It also more briefly surveys social and political crisis tendencies and touches on some popular bourgeois social and political crisis theories. Chapter 2 surveys the neo-orthodox Marxist theory of economic crisis and also so-called "class struggle" crisis theory. It is shown that Marxist theory is based on a more concrete level of capitalist society than market theory, namely, social labor and social-class relationships. Emphasis is given to the theory of labor exploitation and its relationship to economic crisis, and the theory of the "contradiction between productive forces and production relationships."

The Marxist value theory of crisis is meant to be a two-edged sword. First, it is a critique of the self-objectification of human

[3] A good account of the crisis theory of the great rebels within economics – Hobson, Schumpeter, and Veblen (whose works are well known and are not discussed in this book) – is Paul Mattick, "Bourgeois economics," *Economic Crisis and Crisis Theory* (London, 1981).

beings within exchange relationships and the labor process, i.e. it is a critique of the capitalist ideology of commodity and capital fetishism. Second, Marxist crisis theory reconstructs the problem of capitalist accumulation and crisis, since it is more "totalistic" than market theory, and since the ways in which it incorporates market theory transform the meaning or status it has in bourgeois economics. However, value theory retains the convention of abstracting from social-cultural life as well as from real individuals, or "real frogs in real gardens." Value theory is the foundation of the traditional or neo-orthodox Marxist world-view which holds that deficits, unemployment, inflation, and other forms of economic disintegration are the result of contradictions inherent in the process of capital "valorization," "self-expanding capital," and especially contradictions between the production and realization of capital arising from the exploitation of labor.

It is important to stress that traditional or neo-orthodox Marxists present their work as a critique of market theory including its reformist Keynesian variants. Neo-orthodox Marxists critique market theory by theorizing the relationship between value production and value realization rather than market relations alone. They critique Keynesian crisis theory by theorizing the relationship between value and surplus-value production (and total revenues and their distribution between social classes) rather than the relationship between physical production capacity and effective demand. Neo-orthodox Marxists also critique neo-Keynesian crisis theory by theorizing the relationship between changes in value and surplus-value production (and changes in revenues and their distribution) rather than the relationship between changes in physical production capacity and changes in investment and consumption spending. Marxist economists are thus better able to understand the movements of capital as a whole in general, and the process of accumulation through economic crisis in particular.

Marxist theorists believe that value relationships based on capitalist-class domination and exploitation of labor are inherently unstable or crisis-ridden, and also that capitalism is inherently crisis-dependent. Economic crisis, however, may be postponed or displaced, for example, by imperialist expansion, the growth of credit money, restructuring of physical production and social relationships between capital and labor, and capital mobility, as well as by state fiscal, monetary, and other policies. A well-known example is the view that current problems of world capitalism are in large part the result of capital overproduction and/or the tendency of the average rate of profit to fall; when this threatens to bring about a general crisis, the dangerous expansion of credit money and "fictitious profits" postpones or displaces that crisis into the political sphere and the state budget, or internationalizes it (for example, through the creation of massive Third World debt).

The strength of neo-orthodox Marxism, however, is also its weakness. Marxist political economists have a powerful method by which to theorize global movements of capital, labor, commodities, credit, and money; at the same time, they have a manifest inability to grasp the social and political implications for real possibilities of social struggles and social movements. The basic reason is that neo-orthodox Marxists regard individuals as personifications of capitalist production forces and relations, competition, and other "categories" of capital, and, in this sense, little separates them from bourgeois economists. The exception to this rule occurs during times of "economic crisis," when individual workers may discard their masks as owners of the "commodity" labor power and reappear on the historical stage as a political class or "class-for-itself." Neo-orthodox Marxists thus define economic crisis in objectivist terms, as ruptures, breakdowns, or disintegration in the labor or capital markets, commodity markets, or production itself. "Social crisis" and "political class struggle" are seen as historical "dependent variables" dancing to the tune of the "independent variable" called economic crisis. Put another way, Marxists have a systems theory of economic crisis and a social and political theory of social crisis and political struggle, maintaining that the latter is dependent on the former. The Communist party is then regarded as the embodiment of organized historical subjectivity and working-class emancipation, which may come about during economic crisis. Such extreme scientism and voluntarism, which have plagued

Western radicalism for a century or more, originate in Victorian objectivist and individualistic (or great man) theories of history, respectively. They are based on the premise that social development is governed "in the last instance" by economic laws, on the one hand, and strong-willed leaders or the "fittest," on the other. In this sense, there is little space separating Marx and Herbert Spencer, both nineteenth-century thinkers. In fact, this premise conflates the theory of the conditions of capitalist accumulation with the theory of capitalist development historically understood, or *a priori* theory with interpretive dialectics.[4]

While bourgeois economists outline surface crisis phenomena, Marxists expose deeper crisis manifestations at the level of social labor and contradictions between capitalist production forces and relationships. However, both "market relations" and "social labor" are, in fact, abstractions at both the social and the theoretical levels. Nowhere in the world are there pure exchange relations or processes of social labor (or value production and circulation) which are not inscribed and structured by cultural, ideological, and other "social productive forces." Culture and ideology are embedded in market and production forces and relations in complex ways – the discovery of which brings us closer to "real history." History and class struggle, therefore, are not structured by movements of social labor and capital alone, nor still less by changes in wages, prices, and profits, or "market forces." They are ambiguously structured by culture and ideology, tradition and fantasy, personality

---

[4] All nineteenth-century social theory – whether Marxist, Durkheimian, or Weberian – lacks any plausible method to combine positivistic and interpretive approaches to history. There is a strong methodological resemblance between Marx's theory of the *conditions* of capital accumulation, Durkheim's theory of the *conditions* of social solidarity, and Weber's theory of the *conditions* of legitimate authority. The historical conditions, hence intellectual conditions, for "post-scientific" theory in the "age of capital" were lacking. Only in the late twentieth-century world revolutionary epoch, i.e. the epoch of "permanent crisis," have "theoretical history" and sound interpretive approaches to theory and practice become possible. In short, the "historical subject" today is not capital as such, but social-cultural labor and production and reproduction relationships (e.g. James O'Connor, *Accumulation Crisis* (Oxford, 1984), chapters 2 and 3).

development, and other social processes which cannot be reduced to material life strictly defined. Put another way, class struggle does not take place within the productive circuit of capital alone, nor still less within the money and commodity circuits (e.g. wage struggle and struggle against inflation). Class struggle takes place within and against cultural, ideological, state, and other imaginary and real structures within which capital organizes itself, and which simultaneously organize the movements of capital.[5] In particular, the variants of crisis theory which equate exploitation, crisis, and class struggle need to be revolutionized to take into account this basic fact. Failure to do so makes a firm grasp of the "concrete totality" of modern capitalism and imperialism as elusive as it was to the successive Internationals of the nineteenth and twentieth centuries.

Social Relations and Social Theory

Chapter 3 of this work is a critical outline of neo-orthodox Marxist and neo-Marxist theories of social and political crisis and their relationship with economic crisis. The neo-orthodox Marxist theory which suggests that social crisis arises from economic crisis when social and political dangers and opportunities are at their highest pitch is explored first. Subsequently, the key elements of modern neo-Marxist theories of social crisis are scrutinized. Special notice is given to the fact that real individuals in historical time and space are defined by most if not all critical theorists and neo-Marxists as personifications of social categories – ascriptive or demographic groups such as women, racial minorities, youth, and the elderly, on the one hand, and "quasi-groups"[6] such as environmentalists and urban movements, on the other. In this way, neo-Marxists retain the convention established within neo-orthodox Marxism of "reifying" the lived experience of real people in real history. However, critical theory and neo-Marxism are less

[5] O'Connor, *Accumulation Crisis, passim.*
[6] This term was coined by Jürgen Habermas, to the best of my knowledge.

abstract than Marxist political economy, hence potentially more useful in the "concrete analysis of concrete situations." Put another way, neo-Marxism at its rare best critically incorporates market theory and value theory in ways which transform their meaning in bourgeois and neo-orthodox Marxist thinking, respectively; it thus comes closer to representing the "concrete totality" (in Karl Kosik's words) of the social, cultural, ideological, and political economic contradictions which constitute the modern crisis.[7] Social theory is the foundation of the world-view which holds that unemployment, inflation, deficits, and other crisis manifestations are the result of contradictions within and between social and political structures and social action within and against developed capitalist social and ideological structures, which are based not only on work and class but also on gender, ethnic, national, and other identities. These identities (including and especially the modern sense of selfhood discussed in chapter 4) combine and recombine in complex ways which transcend reductionist science as well as individualistic and subjectivistic interpretations of the "present as history."

Social theory at its best defines the modern crisis not only in terms of market relations and production forces and relationships, but also and more importantly in terms of popular interpretations of these categories, including dominant cultural symbols, lived ideologies, political illusions, family relations, and so on. The main tenet of social theory is that there is no such thing as an "economy" defined in either bourgeois or neo-orthodox Marxist terms, hence no "economic crisis" strictly defined, hence, in turn, no theory of economic crisis. Instead, there is a theory of social and political crisis and struggle, which are and are not part and parcel of economic crisis and economic struggle. Both neo-orthodox Marxism and those neo-Marxist conventions which separate economic and social crisis in the form of "systems theory" and "action

[7] Social theory is thus a "critique of the critique" which value theory makes of market theory. It is a "dialectic of non-identity," hence open-ended and inherently self-critical.

theory" are inadequate. The critique of the well-established dualism between objectivist and subjectivist approaches to crisis theory is based on the idea that modern economic, social, political, and cultural crisis interpenetrate one another in ways which transform them into different dimensions of the same historical process – the disintegration and reintegration of the modern world. It is also based on the idea that both neo-orthodox Marxism and many varieties of neo-Marxism mistakenly view the working class and/or particular social groups as merely crisis victims, who may or may not fight back, depending on whether or not neo-orthodox Marxist-Leninist parties and neo- and post-Marxist social movements succeed in their different projects of "enlightenment." The critique of this view is based on the claim that the working class, social and cultural movements, the state, and society as a whole are themselves implicated in the development of the forms and contents of the modern crisis.[8]

Personality Relations and Social Psychological Theory

Chapter 4 of this book is a provisional account of modern personality crisis and its relationship to social and economic crisis trends and the "politics of crisis." The premise of this chapter is that the most concrete level of social life is the day-to-day lived experiences of real "social" individuals. Everyday thoughts, feelings, and actions are more often than not accepted matter-of-factly, but within the context of personality crisis they may also be creatively innovated in self-conscious or unselfconscious ways, hence filled with uncertainty, surprise, real and false hopes and disappointments. It is argued that personality organization includes forms of pyschological repression, sublimation, and projection which guard against individual self-knowledge, and also more transparent views and experiences of capitalist alienation, exploitation, and reification. Psychological repression also (it is argued) distorts

[8] O'Connor, *Accumulation Crisis, passim.*

communication between the inner parts of individual personalities as well as between individuals and groups. In this
sense, personality organization includes the social and cultural
processes of the production and evolution of experience and
meaning (not only fact and knowledge) as well as inner
personality conflicts and struggle.

This suggestive account of personality crisis is meant to be a
critique of the self-deceptions which individuals use to
legitimate to themselves as self-defined moral beings the deceptions of others. It is also an exploratory account of the nature of
modern repression, including forms of distorted communication; it thus explores possibilities of successful social integration into the structures of modern capitalism. Chapter 4
analyzes the relationship between confused social integration
based on repression of affect, unresolved inner conflicts, and
distorted self-knowledge, on the one hand, and communication,
social and system integration, and economic crisis, on the
other. Finally, this chapter offers some suggestions regarding
individual struggles against ideological individualistic identities
and for a richer social identity, explaining how struggles against
repressed affect are both causes and consequences of the
development of a "social individuality." It is stressed, in
particular, that personality crisis is essential for the development of a social individuality, and that redefinitions of the self
as a social being presuppose the successful resolution of personality crisis. Also mentioned is the relationship between
struggles for social individuality and the social construction of
"crisis" as struggles within and against the capitalist state and
political apparatus. This suggests that political struggle and its
relationship to personality struggle should be defined not only
in terms of means to material or social ends but also as ends in
and of themselves. In this way, the old dreams of politics as the
vehicle for the good and just life, and individual identity as the
vehicle of moral and rational as well as expressive and aesthetic
public life, might be reintroduced into crisis theory in useful
ways.

It is hoped that this tentative account of personality crisis will
help theorists and others convert their thought and action from
nineteenth-century *a priori* theory and practice into more

interpretive and action-orientated theories of capitalist accumulation and crisis understood in terms of the present historical
conjuncture of crisis forces and trends. It should be stressed that
this conversion is not and cannot be merely cognitive or
conceptual in nature but also must touch on the emotional
make-up of the theorist. In this sense, this work is meant to have
some personal therapeutic value, while pointing in the direction
of new political orientations and practice. In sum, the purpose is
to develop a method of philosophy of *praxis* which grasps the
personal simultaneously as and as not the political, thus
avoiding "black hole" and traditional dualistic approaches to
the problem of the individual and society. This seems to be a
worthwhile task at a time when the future as history promises
vast changes in all fields of life – both horrific possibilities and
renewed hopes for humankind.

1

Modern Capitalist Crisis and Crisis Theory

Introduction

Many historians regard World War I and the Russian Revolution as the great watershed between the Age of Capital and the Age of Revolution, or the genesis of the crisis of the modern world. Many economists and political scientists believe that the modern crisis deepened during the depression and rise of fascism in the 1920s and 1930s and temporarily culminated in World War II and the Chinese Revolution. In the South and East, anti-colonialism and national liberation struggles and Russian interventions in eastern Europe kept alive the image of the twentieth century as the "century of permanent crisis." However, despite the Cold War, two decades of "peace and prosperity" after World War II eradicated memories of depression, war, and revolution in the minds of many if not most people in the West. These twenty or so years are seen by some Western scholars as an interregnum between the horrors of fascism and world war and a revived crisis, signs of which began to appear in the 1960s. The signs included renewed cycles of national liberation struggles, especially in Southeast Asia; movements of oppressed minorities, students, women, environmentalists, and others in the 1960s and 1970s; worker revolts and rebellions in the late 1960s and early 1970s; and related movements and struggles. Today, these include the growing domination of Japan in the world economy; revolutions and counter-revolutions in southern Africa and Central America; civil war in such countries as Sri Lanka, the Philippines, and

14

Ethiopia; permanent war in the Middle East; religious fundamentalist movements in Iran and India (among other countries); state and private terrorism; and a revival of social agitation and new right-wing, racist, and neo-fascist movements in western Europe and the USA. Last but not least, crisis signs today include the acceleration of the arms race and the new Cold War.

This lexography is appealing because it equates the modern crisis of capitalism and imperialism with twentieth-century history – a century in which the masses of the world for the first time began to shape their own destiny. However, a number of historians have challenged crucial aspects of the "conventional" view. One "revisionist" line is that World War I was as much a crisis of the old system of European empires as it was a war of imperialist rivalry. Another is that the Russian Revolution was as much a restoration of strong statist power in a weak imperialist country as it was a socialist revolution. Still another is that the Great Depression was less the first crisis of modern capitalism and more the last crisis of "classical" capitalism. Another is that fascism was as much the result of the weakness of Germany and Italy in world capitalist economy (and also the result of undeveloped capitalist class structures in which stable bourgeois democratic forms were not possible) as it was a "solution" to traditional capital–labor struggles. A last is that World War II was first and foremost a war against fascism and only secondarily a war of imperialist rivalry between the Allied and Axis powers.

In sum, it is plausible that the *modern* crisis of capitalism began in the 1960s rather than in 1914–17, and hence that the crisis today represents a sharp break with earlier crisis trends between World War I and the cultural, social, and political explosions of two decades or so ago. This formulation of the problem illuminates our experiences during the past twenty years in a number of ways. First, it helps to provide a framework within which we can understand such novel features of the 1960s and 1970s as youth and environmental movements and struggles against bureaucracy, especially the global construction of counter-hegemonic theory, practice, and culture with its emphasis on "quality of life" and the rights of blacks, women, and other ascriptive and quasi-ascriptive groups.[1] Second, it is consistent with the most basic facts of late twentieth-century life – the rise of Japan and China; the full integration of the Third World into the global market; the internationalization, concentration, and centralization of capitalist production; worldwide proletarianization and the development of a "new" middle class or salariat in the older industrial democracies; state interventionism in economic and social life and the creation of the "social factory," or the systemic integration of production and consumption; a tendency toward a permanent military capitalism in most if not all regions in the capitalist world system; the failures of "really existing socialism," and so on. Third, this formulation provides a certain optimism that we are not merely passing through recycled versions of events which occurred earlier in the century; thus it compels us critically to examine traditional economic social theories and political formulae and slogans. Put another way, it helps to explain why there has been a veritable explosion of new empirical and theoretical work on the subject of "crisis" since the mid-1960s.

This crisis literature originally converged on problems of defining "crisis" and identifying crisis symptoms. Economists defined the economic crisis in terms of inflation, unemployment, and stagnation; swollen government deficits and high interest rates; high energy costs and productivity shortfalls; the decline of "smokestack" industries; the inability of national governments to control money supplies;[2] international monetary disequilibria; explosively high Third World debt; and threats of a world credit collapse. Political scientists identified crisis sources in failures of political leadership; weaknesses in crisis management systems; "ungovernability" and "excessive democracy;" the inability of political party systems to channel and control social conflict; and dangerous fault lines in the

---

[1] George Katsiaficas, *The Imagination of the New Left* (Boston, Mass., 1984).

[2] Unregulated Eurodollars amounted to almost $1 trillion in 1984, or just under one-half of the total US money supply.

international political system,[3] especially the revival of strong US intervention in revolutionary civil wars in the Third World and the restoration of the nuclear arms race. Sociologists discovered new and growing social inequalities; rifts in "structures of normative action;" challenges to traditional authority; "deficits" of motivations and incentives; "insufficiencies of social control"; and a revival of atomized individualism. Psychologists became increasingly alarmed by the "crisis of the family," especially the plague of divorce, family violence, and child abuse, as well as other signs of social decadence such as violent pornography, widespread drug abuse, increased crime, and what at least a few regard as a trend toward mass personality disintegration and social and political fanaticism. Only a few professional cheerleaders affirmed traditional ideologies of individualism and personal success, and predicted a future economic boom and social and political wellbeing.[4] By contrast, many traditional social scientists recognized that there had emerged a "crisis" in the Western idea of progress itself, which some regarded as both cause and effect of the general crisis of the modern world.[5]

Signs of Economic Crisis

Economists found abundant evidence consistent with their definitions and explanations of economic crisis. Most believed that modern capitalism is an international system of produc-

---

[3] Sir Peter Hill-Norton, "Crisis management," *NATO Review*, 5 (October 1976).

[4] Herman Kahn, *The Coming Boom: Economic, Political, and Social* (New York, 1982).

[5] Gabriel A. Almond, Marvin Chodorow, and Roy Harvey Pearce, *Progress and its Discontents* (Berkeley, Cal., 1982). Allan Wilson, a University of California biochemist, offers the most extreme naturalistic theory of the "decline of progress" – namely, that the human species has become imitative, not innovative, because the development of the human brain has short-circuited genetic evolution. "I'm afraid we've reached a plateau and that Homo sapiens is in a nose dive" (quoted in *San Francisco Examiner*, July 29, 1984).

tion, distribution, exchange, and consumption, hence that economic crisis tendencies are worldwide in scope. This means that the point of departure of crisis theory should be the specific conjunctural circumstances of world capitalism today. It is widely agreed that the crisis affects different parts of world economy in different ways; for example, austerity social budgets and youth unemployment appear to be universal; relocation of productive facilities, industrial stagnation, and low rates of capitalist accumulation are confined to certain older industrial regions; semi-peripheral or sub-imperialist countries such as Mexico and South Africa are appropriating a larger share of the global surplus.[6] Many observers believe that crisis tendencies in the US "rust belt" were especially severe because of the decline of US political and military hegemony in the world system in the 1960s and 1970s and associated international economic, financial, and political disorder. "The proper functioning of [the world capitalist] system requires a well-organized and universally accepted hierarchy of political and military authority and responsibility among the nations of the system."[7] This hierarchy, with the USA at its head since the end of World War II, is believed to have been undermined by new developments in technology, communications, transport, and global labor supplies which have resulted in the relocation of industrial

---

[6] Immanuel Wallerstein, "Semi-peripheral countries and the contemporary world crisis," *Theory and Society*, 3, 4 (Winter 1976), 464.

[7] James R. Crotty, "Lifeline for capitalism," *The Progressive* (January 1979), 49, citing Robert Heilbroner, *Beyond Boom and Crash* (New York, 1978).

The problem with this approach is that it fails to grasp the problem by using the method of combined and uneven development, but rather uses a method which studies "national rivalries" and relations between international capital and nation-states. For Marxist versions of this approach, see Harry Magdoff and Paul M. Sweezy, "The dollar crisis: what next?", in *The End of Prosperity: The American Economy in the 1970s* (New York, 1977), and Ernest Mandel, *Decline of the Dollar: A Marxist View of the Monetary Crisis* (New York, 1972).

The classical account of the failure of the USA to abide by the rules of the international economic system it created, thus threatening international economic chaos, is Fred Block, *The Origins of International Economic Disorder* (Berkeley, Cal., 1979).

facilities to low-wage regions of the world, hence that the "crisis" in the developed world is the result of a new international division of labor.

Nevertheless, most if not all Third World countries, including the "newly industrializing countries", suffered deep trauma when the world recession of the early 1980s reduced raw material prices and export earnings, forcing governments to cut back needed imports and fall more deeply into external debt. Real per capita income in the Third World as a whole fell by about 8 per cent between 1980 and 1984. More significant for workers and peasants, production destined for the home market (including subsistence agriculture) declined and capital-intensive production for export markets increased. The Third World was racked by growing sectoral and regional imbalances and distortions, meanwhile deprived of even the semblance of nationally determined economic policies, being "overwhelmingly oriented to the world market."[8] The decline in the global inflation rate beginning in late 1981 was small compensation for increasing unemployment, underemployment, and poverty in the underdeveloped countries. In countries such as Brazil, where new austerity programs caused prices of foodstuffs and other necessities to skyrocket (in Brazil, inflation increased by well over 100 per cent in 1983, while real gross national production declined),[9] declining world inflation rates were no compensation at all.

External debt in many Third World countries grew dramatically during the 1980s.[10] In the Third World as a whole, foreign debt reached an unbelievable $750–800 billion in 1983 – almost one-half of which was owed to private banks.[11] In Latin

[8] Folker Froebel, Jürgen Heinrichs, and Otto Kreye, "The global crisis and developing countries," Starnberg Institute for the Study of Global Structures, Developments, and Crises, MS, undated, 6–8.

[9] Marcos Arruda et al., "Economic dictatorship versus democracy in Brazil," *Latin American Perspectives*, 11, 1 (Winter 1984), 40.

[10] Darrel Dalamaide, *Debt Shock* (New York, 1984).

[11] Good surveys of the international debt issue include Duncan Cameron, "Order and disorder in the world economy: international finance in evolution," *Studies in Political Economy*, 11 (Summer 1983); Robert E. Wood, "Making sense of the debt crisis: a primer for socialists," *Socialist Review* (15,

America, the average payment to meet interest charges on external debt amounted to almost 40 per cent of export earnings. Newly industrializing countries such as South Korea regarded world debt (together with high interest rates and currency misalignments) as the greatest barrier to economic expansion.[12] Mainstream economists believed that this tragedy and the dangers of a world financial collapse were the result of factors other than merely the effects of world recession on Third World export earnings. One was the huge backlog of loans to the underdeveloped and "developing countries" financed by recycled petrodollars after the "oil shocks" of 1973 and 1979. Another was the expansion of the US military budget "to provide the military strength and political security to ensure peace in the world" (in President Reagan's words), which drove up Federal budgetary deficits, interest rates, and absorbed a larger share of world savings. The dollar was thus strengthened by the flow of short-term capital from western Europe and other regions into the USA, which increased Third World debt burdens even more (80 per cent of Third World loans were in dollars). Finally, new protectionist tendencies in the First World and sluggish socialist economies made it more difficult for underdeveloped and "developing countries" to expand export earnings in order to repay their debt.

Adrift internally in a sea of red ink, the US government used the International Monetary Fund to try to force Brazil, Mexico, Argentina, Morocco, Tunisia, the Philippines, and other countries into black ink in their external accounts. The weapons used were "austerity programs," which lowered real wages and

---

3), 81 (May–June 1985); "The two faces of Third World debt," *Monthly Review* (January 1984).

[12] Yet, ironically, it is precisely because of Third World debt that the USA, western Europe, and Japan are more dependent on Third World imports than they are on imports from one another. Japan, for example, sells over 50 per-cent of its exports to the Third World. There is thus a close connection between the relocation of industry, developed-country loans to the Third World, Third World debt, and First World export potentials (André Gundar Frank, "Policy ad hockery: unemployment and world crisis of economic policy formation," paper delivered at Round Table '83, Marxism and the World Today, Cavtat, Yugoslavia (October 1983), 8).

incomes in Third World countries, creating the now infamous "International Monetary Fund riots." However, programs to cut back imports, starve industry producing for domestic markets, increase unemployment, and aggressively push Third World export industries became a formula for deepening, not remedying world recession, as well as for a revival of militarism. By 1984 more Third World countries were demanding that the IMF and Western banks renegotiate their external debt. The result was not only a sharp decline in bond prices and the value of bank stocks in the USA, but also threats to the stability of the world banking system itself.[13]

In the developed capitalist countries, more crisis signs appeared during the 1970s and first half of the 1980s. In the USA, western Europe, and Japan, during the 1960s and most of the 1970s, profit rates and profit shares of national income declined [14] (selectivity improving in restructured industries such as automobiles in the 1980s). In the last half of the 1970s, corporate profits (adjusted for inflation) in the USA were no more than those prevailing a decade earlier. However, statistics

---

[13] Manufacturers Hanover Bank's loans to four countries (Mexico, Brazil, Argentina, and Venezuela) totaled $6.3 billion at the end of 1983, or 10 percent of the bank's total assets. Citicorp had $10.2 billion in outstanding loans to these countries, 7.6 percent of its assets. Chase Manhattan, Chemical New York, Morgan Guarantee Trust, Bankers Trust, Bank of America, and Wells Fargo were not far behind.

"The nine biggest banks in the US have lent to risky countries in South America and elsewhere sums amounting to more than 250 per cent of their capital and reserves. If less than half of this money were to prove irrecoverable, they would be without any capital at all": Harold Lever, "The debt won't be paid," *The New York Review*, June 28, 1984, 3. Lever (among many other writers) has made a good case that most of these loans cannot and will not be repaid. He also stressed the important role of the US government in encouraging the unrelenting expansion of foreign loans as a way to support or prop up its political allies.

[14] Between 1958 and 1976 it was estimated that changes in the rate of profit in industry in the USA, Great Britain, Germany, and Japan were −2.0 percent, −4.1 per cent, −2.9 per cent, and −2.4 per cent, respectively (S. H. Heap, "World profitability crisis in the 1970s: some empirical evidence," *Capital and Class*, 11 (1980–81); Samuel Bowles and Herbert Gintis, "The crisis of liberal democratic capitalism: the case of the United States," *Politics and Society*, 11, 1 (1982), 54 table 1).

on average profits and profit rates concealed significant variations between economic sectors. In the USA, profit growth rates between 1973 and 1980 in traditional industries and agriculture declined; high-technology industries were favored by moderate increases; and the energy and service sectors (particularly banking and finance, which benefited from big differentials between inflation and interest rates) enjoyed handsome increases in profit growth rates.[15]

These figures suggested to some economists that there was a general crisis of capitalism in which the energy and financial sectors protected themselves by increasing rents and bank profits at the expense of industry and agriculture. Other economists believed that there was merely a shift in the focus of economic activity, or changes in the regional and international division of labor. Some economists in the first camp believed that world capitalism had entered a new downswing of a "long wave" of accumulation in a milieu of sharply increased international competition. By the mid-1980s, there were more warnings of the possibility of a massive global depression. Economists in the second camp believed that economic growth and high levels of employment in corporate administration, services, research and development, and related fields, as well as high-technology industries and consumer services in the developed countries, together with economic prosperity in Japan and most if not all "newly industrializing countries," suggested that the modern crisis was sectoral and regional in nature.[16] Still

---

[15] "America's restructured economy," *Business Week*, June 1, 1981. *Business Week* stressed the danger of various economic sectors "spinning apart," i.e. that "the latest investment surge in the US economy did not lead to cost reductions."

In the early 1980s, agriculture was in the worst condition since the 1930s. Only large-scale farms with low debt prospered. In 1981, 1 percent of all farms appropriated two-thirds of all farm profits.

[16] The literature on regional and international shifts in economic activity in general and the problem of "reindustrialization" in particular is vast. Hunter Lewis and Donald Allison (*The Real World War* (New York, 1984)) documented the loss of world market shares by the USA to other industrial countries and argued that the USA has ignored many economic opportunities, counseling a highly nationalistic economic policy of export expansion. See also Robert Z. Lawrence, *Can America Compete?* (Washington, DC, 1984);

others argued that the "crisis" was resolved by the mid-1980s – at least from the standpoint of the giant, conglomerate, international corporations whose high profits indicated good, not bad, economic times.[17]

However, even those economists who believed in the existence of a general crisis of capitalism agreed that the internationalization of capitalist production by transnational corporations reinforced the long-term structural shift in the USA (and to a lesser degree western Europe) away from traditional industry to finance and administration, corporate services, commerce, and so on, and high-technology industries.[18] This thesis was born out by the following facts. Although total investment in relation to gross national product in the USA (for example) remained within the 10 per cent range from the 1950s through the end of the 1970s, spending on new plants and equipment (excluding agriculture) fell drastically during the 1980–82 recession, when investment in comparison with new national product was at its lowest level since the end of World War II. Furthermore, the long-run trend indicated a larger proportion of investment spending in trade and commerce, finance and real estate, services, and communications and high-technology equipment.[19] For example, the stock of capital grew by about one-third between 1970 and 1978.[20] But the composition of investment in equipment shifted towards communications and high-technology production (e.g.

Ira C. Magaziner and Robert B. Reich, *Minding America's Business: The Decline and Rise of the American Economy* (New York, 1982); S. M. Miller and Donald Tomaskovic-Devey, *Recapitalizing America: Alternatives to the Corporate Distortion of National Policy* (Boston, Mass., 1982).

[17] Frederick F. Clairmonte and John H. Cavanagh, "Global capitalism: the dynamics of the top 200," MS, undated.

[18] There was also wide agreement that the internationalization of production reinforced the international synchronization of the short-term capitalist business cycle.

[19] "Are low savings ruining the US economy?", *Monthly Review* (December 1980), table 4, 9; "Supply-side theory and capital investment," *Monthly Review* (April 1983).

[20] "Reagan and the nemesis of inflation," *Monthly Review* (January 1981). In 1980 the investment ratio was actually somewhat higher than it was in 1950, 1960, or 1970.

office machinery, medical equipment, and the like). Moreover, the composition of investment in structures shifted toward commercial building, mining, and oil drilling.[21] In short, the US economy (and to a lesser degree the advanced economies of western Europe) was increasingly specializing in corporate administration, finance and real estate, commerce, services, etc., and simultaneously automating these sectors together with old-line industry, where productivity increased sharply in the 1980s with the increased use of new high-technology products.

Many economists believed that shifts in the regional and international division of labor were not only correlated with but also responsible for declining productivity and increased unit labor costs in the 1960s and 1970s.[22] Other factors which (some said) contributed to lower productivity included increases in unit costs in construction because of a shift from industrial construction to housing; shortfalls in mining productivity because of government safety regulations together with a shift to higher-cost coal operations; lower productivity in utilities because of the failure of nuclear plants to deliver cheap energy; and slower growth of energy demand because of the

[21] "Supply-side theory and capital investment." While the investment ratio has remained more or less constant, the growth rate of both producer durable goods and non-residential structures has declined more or less steadily between 1958–65 and 1980–82. Investment in communications and high-tech equipment has not been strong enough to sustain the growth rate of investment in equipment as a whole. Similarly, investment in commercial structures, mining, and oil drilling has not been strong enough to keep up the growth rate in non-residential structures as a whole (ibid.).

[22] In the USA between 1960 and 1973, average productivity grew by only 2.5 percent annually. In Britain, Germany, and Japan, productivity growth was 4 percent, 6 per cent, and 10 percent, respectively. The reason often given is that US capital has internationalized production at a more rapid rate than its rivals. In the USA since 1965, productivity growth rates have declined. In the late 1970s, the USA was the only industrial country in which productivity growth was slightly negative; the 3.5 percent increase in (non-agricultural) productivity in the "recovery" of 1983 was the slowest growth rate in any expansion period on record since World War II. It is generally agreed that this did *not* occur because investment in relation to total product declined. According to *Business Week*, annual productivity growth slipped from 1.5 percent between 1969 and 1979 to 1.3 percent in 1979–85 (*Business Week*, September 16, 1985).

development of energy-saving techniques in industry in the 1970s and the recession of the early 1980s (hence a growth of unused capacity and high-cost energy outputs). In addition, the use of rising profit margins (mainly a form of ground rent) by energy companies for acquisitions and mergers,[23] together with older industrial capital's obsession with diversification and protection rather than expansion of profits (hence its refusal to lay out money for expansion investments), were seen by many as basic reasons why productivity (particularly in manufacturing) remained relatively stagnant in the 1970s and early 1980s. Another frequently heard argument was that US industry was destroyed by the costs of empire, or the diversion of money capital needed for industrial restructuring to military spending.

Low productivity growth, together with rising energy costs, among other factors, led to growing inflation in the late 1970s and early 1980s, which damaged the economy by encouraging investment in low-risk, quick-return projects, including increasing speculation. Another result of low productivity was high real interest rates, which in addition were caused by growing Federal government deficits and tight monetary policy, lower levels of investment in financial assets, and the appearance of a dangerously unbalanced financial structure, which was increasingly inflated by the expansion of credit advanced to save failing banks and to avoid financial panic.[24]

By the mid-1970s there were unmistakable signs of an investment strike in basic industries in the USA and some European countries.[25] At any given operating rate in US

---

[23] In 1980 "natural resource companies" accounted for over 40 percent of mergers (*Dollars and Sense* (December 1981), 4).

[24] Total US debt of individuals, business, and governments grew from c.$1 trillion in 1965 to c.$2.4 trillion in 1975 to c.$7.2 trillion in 1985 (Leonard Silk, "Economic scene," *The New York Times*, January 18, 1985).

[25] During the "recovery" of 1976, for example, industrial construction in the USA failed to reach two-thirds of 1969 levels ("The danger in the plan consumption slump," *Business Week*, April 5, 1976, 25). Reasons given included more efficient plant design, rising construction costs, and declines in expected profits. Meanwhile, speculation intensified. The big conglomerates bought up companies already established in profitable lines of business rather

manufacturing industries, large corporations were laying out increasingly less capital in new productive capacity.[26] As noted above, however, by the early 1980s, as a result of austerity programs and successful attacks against the labor, environmental, and other movements, profits showed signs of recovering from the lows of the 1960s and 1970s. In the USA, even during the final years of the Carter administration, profits were growing three times as fast as new capital investment, yet industrial production was expanding only by fits and starts. While the USA posted the best economic record of all the advanced capitalist countries in the late 1970s, the large corporations continued to wait for a better social and political climate for long-run profitability.[27]

The capital strike in older industries, together with slower economic growth, inflation, higher interest rates, and other factors, resulted in reductions in living standards for many. In the USA, despite increases in money wages, inflation and taxation began to reduce real wages and salaries in some branches of the economy as early as the late 1960s. The structural shift to low-wage trade and service sectors helped to depress the average wage rate. While median family income from 1950 to 1970 rose by two-thirds, between 1970 and 1979 family income increased by only 6 per cent, and thereafter declined. Meanwhile, worsening economic conditions, combined with the fiscal crisis, "legitimated" the reduction of Federal spending on social services in the late 1970s and

---

than building new facilities and expanding capacity. Pension funds formed real-estate pools to purchase office buildings and shopping centres which were already built and profitably rented ("Pension money diversifies into real estate," *Business Week*, January 20, 1975). Corporations reduced spending on new raw material exploration and production and also on research and development ("The silent crisis in R & D," *Business Week*, March 8, 1976).

[26] This is indicated by the "Eickhoff Curve" which shifted steadily downward from 1954 to 1969, 1970 to 1976, and 1973 to 1976 ("The Eickhoff Curve," *Wall Street Journal*, April 4, 1977).

[27] In this period, the economic growth of industrial rivals was mainly due to the expansion of their overseas business operations. The US economy grew because the domestic economy expanded.

1980s.[28] Big capital forced many unions to accept pay cuts and "take backs" and employed more "illegal workers," whose wages were below average and whose labor power was more "exploitable" because of the absence of trade-union and governmental regulation of safety conditions, job structures, and pay scales. By 1980, big business's huge contributions to anti-union, right-wing political candidates through corporate Political Action Committees and "New Right" political efforts began to pay high dividends. The profits of many restructured large corporations grew, and the political and ideological terrain became increasingly defined in terms of "Reaganism," a contradictory mixture of neo-liberalism, neo-conservatism, and neo-individualism,[29] with a heavy dose of "military Keynesian" deficit spending thrown in for good measure.

Within the industrial world, the European Economic Community slid into third place behind the USA and Japan in the world economic sweepstakes. This was partly the result of particular internal problems in Britain, West Germany, and France, and of European conservatism following the first "oil shock" of 1973–74. A do-nothing policy during the mid-1970s was followed by half a decade of new government incentives to modernize older industry and introduce energy-saving technology, which, however, failed to have positive economic results. As a result of these and other failures, in Britain, West Germany, France (governed by a "socialist" Prime Minister and Cabinet), and many other countries, there was a political shift to the right and a revival of economic liberalism. Social budgets were cut back; the tenuous unity between Socialist and Communist parties was weakened; and most if not all European countries began to rely on the "pull of the market" rather than the "push of government incentives" to restore economic growth.

In the USA, big capital's economic offensive against

---

[28] James O'Connor, "The fiscal crisis of the state revisited," *Kapitalistate*, 9 (1981). *Total* spending on social programs declined less, mainly because state governments picked up some of the slack, and also because Congress restored some of the 1981–82 budget cuts in 1983 and 1984.

[29] James O'Connor, *Accumulation Crisis* (Oxford, 1984), chapter 8.

organized labor, women, ethnic minorities, the elderly, the urban poor, and the environmental movement was strengthened by intensified ideological warfare against government regulation of industry, occupational health and safety, "liberal" forms of public education, racial integration, and feminism, including feminist struggles for unionization and equal and comparable pay. Meanwhile, in the workplace there were more speed-ups and lay-offs. In the early 1980s, strikes declined, resistance by unions to threats to the social security system weakened, opposition to indexing wages and social security and other transfer payments grew. President Reagan's National Labor Relations Board in effect began to attack the principle of collective bargaining and the right of workers to engage in collective action. In the cities, the "informal economy" mushroomed, and "home work" organized by capital reduced wages, fringe benefits, and spending on safe working conditions.

Last but not least, large-scale capital was able to continue to disperse the working class geographically through regionalization of production and decentralization of operating units to small towns and rural areas.[30] In the USA, between 1970 and 1980, rural areas grew faster than metropolitan regions for the first time in history.[31] Between 1976 and 1982, 62 per cent of new plants were established in the Southern USA. In the North Central states and the Northeast, the proportion of new plants in relation to all new productive facilities fell from 24 per cent

[30] Plant closures in the older industrial zones appear to have been mainly due to long-run processes of capital restructuring rather than the 1981–82 recession, according to research on California by Amy Glasmeier. Yet the increasingly severe recessions of the 1970s and early 1980s hit the older, highly specialized industrial regions relatively harder than other regions – which doubtless encouraged more plant closures, disinvestment, and relocation.

[31] *New York Times*, March 3, 1981. Population growth in rural areas was 15.4 percent; in urban areas, only 9.1 percent. Urban population declined by 2 percent in the Northeast and rose by only 1.6 percent in the Midwest. Meanwhile, rural population grew by 12.4 percent and 7.8 percent, respectively. In the West, urban population growth was 21.2 percent, but rural growth was 31.8 percent. Only in the South was urban growth greater than rural expansion – 20.1 percent and 17.1 percent, respectively.

to 15 per cent and from 13 per cent to 11 per cent, respectively (the West's relative position remained unchanged).[32] The main reasons included higher worker productivity, more efficient transportation and less congestion, lower ground rents and taxes, cheaper wages and energy costs, and a better business climate in general. Meanwhile, as has been noted, industry in Japan and a handful of Third World countries, mainly concentrated in East Asia, grew at the expense of older industry in the USA and western Europe. The overall logic of these trends was that in past decades the traditional geographic centralization of industry and population (i.e. urbanization) helped to expand markets, hence to realize values and profits more easily. At present, decentralization and dispersion of industry and population help to increase labor discipline and productivity and in other ways lower costs, hence to produce values and profits more efficiently.

The result of these efforts oriented (to use Marxist terms) to the problem of restoring capital's domination of the working class and expanding profits was an increase in absolute surplus value, a reduction in the size of the average consumption basket and social wage, and perhaps a decline in the value content of the average consumption basket and social services – in short, a sharp increase in the rate of exploitation. Austerity policies, of course, had differential effects on different fractions of the working class and salariat in the private and public sectors. "New middle-class" income in high-technology industries, research and development, corporate administration, finance, and related sectors of the economy increased even during the recession of the 1980s. At the other end of the income distribution, maintenance of consumption levels, especially in older industries and agriculture, depended on workers sinking deeper into debt or supplying more family members or work hours to the labor market to maintain or increase family income.[33]

---

[32] Cited in *San Jose Mercury*, June 3, 1982.
[33] Elliot Currie, Robert Dunn, and David Fogarty, "The new immiseration," *Socialist Review*, 54 (10, 6) November–December 1980), 12–13; Lester Thurow, "More are going to be poor," *The New Republic*, November

However, these strategies for maintaining family consumption levels became increasingly less effective, particularly among black workers. The result was a trend toward economic polarization – increased inequalities in income distribution and absolute and relative declines in the income of blacks and the poor.[34] More or less a majority of North Americans and western Europeans experienced the crisis in the form of lowered real consumption and living conditions. Deregulation, decentralization of industry, and productivity drives meant that many if not most workers also suffered deteriorating work and health and safety conditions.

Despite new efficiency initiatives in industry, capital restructuring, reductions in family consumption standards, declines in the quantity and quality of social services, and unemployment, economic pundits and policymakers stated that (in Marxist terms) the rate of exploitation needed to be pushed higher to increase profits sufficiently to stimulate a strong renewal of investment, production, and employment. "This country is in the process of discovering that it can no longer afford the big life," Leonard Gross wrote in the mid-1970s. "Gains in real income for the middle class have been tiny; there's almost no upward mobility any longer. . . . There will be practical changes in the way people live: smaller, less elaborate houses, fewer single-family dwellings, more cluster zoning, more condominiums, better use of land space to provide more recreation near the home."[35] The ideological task was to convince the average family that "less is more" and to "diminish discontent by reordering priorities." After the 1979 "oil shock," Paul Volcker, Chairman of the Federal Reserve Bank, stated that "the standard of living of the American people has to

---

2, 1974, 26–7. It needs to be stressed that real per capita income actually rose by 28 percent between 1970 and 1983.

[34] Between 1980 and 1984, the income of the most affluent one-fifth of US families rose by almost 9 percent; that of the poorest one-fifth declined by nearly 8 percent: John L. Palmer and Isabel V. Sawhill (eds), *The Reagan Record* (New York, 1984), 320.

[35] "Is less more?", *Newsweek*, July 14, 1975.

decline."[36] Charles Schultze, head of the President's Council of Economic Advisors at the time, "agreed emphatically."[37] President Jimmy Carter added that "discipline" and "pain" were essential to restore a healthy economy. The strictest kind of monetarist policy was introduced in the USA and Britain in 1979, resulting in two years of world monetary contraction, with effects ranging from "disinflation" to "deflation," especially with regard to Third World raw material prices. While presidential candidate Ronald Reagan derided Carter's pessimistic economic prognosis, President Reagan cut tens of billions from the Federal social budget; pushed a regressive tax cut through the Congress; attempted with some success to strip workers and consumers of governmental protection of work conditions, the environment, and consumer products; and in 1981–82 plunged the economy into the worst recession in forty years as the price of ending double-digit inflation and moderating interest rates.[38]

Bourgeois Views of Economic Crisis

Reagan government policies were developed and implemented in the name of neo-classical and monetarist economic theory, which became the dominant bourgeois theories of crisis by the 1980s. Liberal Democrats protested that Reagan and Federal Reserve Bank policies were responsible for economic hard times.[39] But most academic and government economists argued

[36] Quoted by Andrew Tully, "Carter's inflation in action," *Santa Cruz Sentinel*, November 1, 1979.

[37] Quoted in *The Economist* (London), October 27, 1979.

[38] In Britain, the neo-liberal policy of engineering a deep recession to discipline labor turned out to be inconsistent with the policy of cutting social spending because high unemployment increased the demand for social entitlements: "Interview with Bob Sutcliffe," *Dollars and Sense* (December 1982). This was true, to a lesser degree, in the USA.

[39] Liberal Democrats argued that the Republicans were guilty of engineering increasingly severe recessions. Peak unemployment during the "Nixon recession" of 1969–70 was 6.1 percent; the "Nixon/Ford recession" of 1973–75, 9 percent; the "Reagan recession" beginning in 1981, nearly 10

that expansionary fiscal and monetary policies, in particular policies to increase government spending and private consumption, no longer offered solutions to crisis trends but rather were capitalism's major problem.[40] Economic policymakers thus rejected Keynesian policies of expanding investment more rapidly than consumption, in favor of a policy of increasing investment at the expense of consumption. In the last years of the 1970s, it was frequently heard in business circles that a reduction in consumption was the precondition not only for more economic "discipline" and "pain" but also for an increase in the rate and mass of profits. "It is now becoming clear that stacking the economic deck against savings and toward more and more current consumption has turned out to be a mistake of monumental proportions."[41] Big capital's spokesmen argued forcibly in favor of reversing consumption-oriented incentives promoted by inflationary expectations, social security payments tied to cost of living, progressive income taxation, and ceilings on interest rates. The attack on consumption logically functioned as a method for creating permanent economic slack, or relatively deep recessions and short-lived and shallow recoveries.[42]

---

percent (Democratic Study Group, US House of Representatives, "Special report: the Reagan recession," No. 97–35, Washington, DC, December 9, 1981). Populist Democrats blamed the Federal Reserve Bank for excruciatingly high interest rates and "retrenchment."

[40] As Stephen Marglin has pointed out, structuralist theories of underdevelopment which called for national economic planning in the Third World went out of favor at exactly the same moment that Keynesian theories of planning in the developed countries were defeated in government and academic circles ("The wealth of nations," *The New York Review*, July 19, 1984).

[41] "The US bias against savings," *Business Week*, December 11, 1978, 90, 92. This theme was constantly reiterated during the 1980s (e.g. Leonard Silk, "Economic scene," *The New York Times*, September 28, 1984).

[42] Consumption, not investment, spending led the way in the economic recovery after 1975. Investment spending itself grew at less than 50 percent of the normal rate in the preceding four major recoveries since World War II despite the fact that the post-1975 profit rate rose faster than the average of past recoveries. The reason was that business was reducing borrowing and trying to restore favorable liquidity conditions. Military spending and (ironically) consumption also led the way in the 1983 recovery.

The growing counter-revolution in big business thinking about economy and society was echoed within mainstream social science. Sociologists argued that in a high-consumption economy traditional impulse controls become unhinged and the work ethic subverted. Social psychologists maintained that balances between work and consumption could be restored only at different and unknown levels of personality integration. Businessmen, especially in Japan where they are famous for perfecting aggressive production and export strategies and methods of keeping down the cost of labor, repeated these arguments in cruder terms.[43] With a wary eye to rapid economic growth in Japan and East Asia, academic economists in the USA joined the counter-revolution in economic theory which in this way gathered more strength in policy-making circles.

The last Keynesian policy proposal designed to expand consumer demand (Carter's proposed $50 tax cut in 1977 to stimulate spending) succumbed to arguments that there were surpluses, not shortages, of effective demand and consumer credit. Thereupon, economists became obsessed with "supply-side economics."[44] They saw "shortages" everywhere – shortages of cheap energy and transportation; of money capital; of incentives to build new productive facilities; of fresh research and development outlays; and of disciplined workers. They stressed the need to raise total investment and to increase the productivity of the existing stock of fixed capital. Increases in investment (it was said) required a redistribution of credit from housing and consumer-durable markets to the capital market. It was broadly hinted that increasing the productivity of fixed capital would have to take place at the expense not only of jobs but also of working conditions and workers' safety and health.

[43] "US is urged to 'put house in order,'" *San Francisco Chronicle*, February 6, 1979. "Quoting from an American research paper on how Japanese leaders perceive the US, [the editor-in-chief of *Japan Economic Journal*] said that 'for several years, [the leaders] have felt that American industry is growing weak and non-competitive, that American workers are habitually lazy....'"

[44] A fine account is James T. Campen and Arthur MacEwan, "Crisis, contradictions, and conservative controversies in contemporary US capitalism," *Review of Radical Political Economics* (*RRPE*) 14, 3 (Fall 1982).

Meanwhile, ecological economists unwittingly strengthened the hands of the neo-classical economists' claim that consumption was too high by pointing to shortages of natural resources and dangerous levels of pollution.

Bourgeois theories of both short-term and long-term crisis trends in effect became obsessed with supply deficits of various kinds. The recessionary turn of 1978 was attributed to shortages of industrial capacity, labor strikes, and a deficiency of oil supplies.[45] Theories of long-term stagflation also highlighted the theme of shortages. Inflation-induced, high-cost money capital was one of the most popular. Another was that growing international competition and the post-war trend towards "capital-deepening" resulted in lower rates of return on new investments, i.e. profit shortfalls. Business needed to rebuild fixed plant along modernized lines; this presupposed a spell of economic hard times during which excess plant could be used up and excess debt eliminated.[46]

The economics profession and the higher business circles largely adopted Milton Friedman and others' argument that inflation was the basic cause of economic distress, and that government deficits, excessive money and credit, high marginal tax rates, and over-regulation of business were the basic source of inflation.[47] The government became the scapegoat for inflation, unemployment, slow economic growth, and other crisis signs. The revived cult of the "entrepreneur" as economic savior highlighted the theme that capitalism itself was "perfect and entire, wanting nothing."

One central argument emphasized the effects of state borrowing on credit availability and interest rates. It was repeated *ad nauseam* that Federal borrowing created a credit squeeze which forced capitalists out of the capital market and also

[45] "Why supply-side economics is suddenly popular," *Business Week*, September 17, 1979.

[46] "New life for Kondratieff's gloomy cycle," *Business Week*, September 10, 1979.

[47] For example, the culprits for Martin Feldstein were the combination of inflation and high marginal tax rates: *Inflation, Tax Rules, and Capital Formation* (Chicago, 1983).

absorbed an excessive share of total savings, which were then returned via debt service to individuals devoted to consumption not saving.[48] Economist-policymakers such as Alan Greenspan believed that expectations in the money market that Federal deficits would continue to grow also caused high long-term interest rates. Other economists were more critical and thoughtful, pointing to the deregulation of the financial sector as a crucial source of high interest rates. Still others (such as Secretary of the Treasury, Donald Regan) claimed that banks were deliberately holding up interest rates to protect themselves against anticipated losses on foreign and domestic loans. Finally, the theory attributing deficits to high interest rates was accompanied by the claim that state employment was inherently "unproductive," hence that state spending and employment should be reduced, meanwhile expanding manufacturing and other "productive" sectors.[49]

Above all, the view was heard that high taxation stifled economic growth. High taxation supposedly created "incentives shortages" within the entrepreneurial, managerial, and professional strata.[50] Lower taxes would create incentives for

[48] This argument ignores the fact that Federal deficits may expand private bank reserves and hence potential money supplies. It also neglects the fact that the state borrows in part to amortize or refinance past loans, with the result that more potential money capital is put into the hands of the capitalists. Last but not least, it ignores the independent effect of private borrowing for speculation and other unproductive uses on interest rates. Harry Magdoff has pointed out to me that between 1981 and 1982 net US government borrowing almost doubled, while interest rates on Treasury bills fell from 14 percent to 10.7 percent (the main reason, of course, being a big decline in private borrowing) (letter, July 22, 1984).

[49] This line of reasoning neglects the indirectly productive role of state workers in such fields as transportation, communications, education, and health. It also mistakenly grasps the concept of "productivity" in technical rather than social terms. Capitalism's problem is not primarily to raise physical output per worker, but rather surplus value production per worker. (A good discussion is Peter Howell's "Once again on productive and unproductive labour," *Revolutionary Communist*, nos 3–4 (November 1975), 46–7).

[50] This argument presupposes that capitalists and their managers cannot find ways around high marginal rates of income taxation which supposedly serve tax equity but which function more or less symbolically. Since World

more people to work harder and longer.[51] Tax cuts would also provide rewards for saving (because of increases in after-tax income on interest and dividends) and investing (because after-tax profit rates would be higher). Tax cuts were thus expected to increase economic growth by raising savings and investment.[52] The specific reason was that reductions in marginal tax rates were expected to be greatest at the highest income levels, tempting the rich and near-rich out of tax shelters and into productive investments. The expected effects of reduced taxation on profits were stressed by both Democratic and Republican political leaders.[53] Finally, some economists argued that social security taxation and benefits were so high that private savings were discouraged.[54]

These views by monetarist and neo-classical economists were underpinned by the dogmatic belief that economic problems in the USA and the rest of the world were remediable through the

---

War II, every US tax reform measure until 1986 has not merely failed, but has been transformed into its opposite, i.e. more loopholes have been created.

[51] "A guide to understanding the supply-siders," *Business Week*, December 22, 1980. "Roberts and his supply-side colleagues argue that cutting marginal tax rates . . . will boost net wages and encourage work through such means as increased overtime, less absenteeism, more part-time work, later retirement, and shorter periods of unemployment. . . . [Robert] Mundell further argues that rising taxes have had so large an inflationary impact on the cost of many goods and services that they have led many people to forgo purchases and perform services themselves that could be more efficiently handled by others . . . underground economic activity . . . says [Arthur] Laffer, . . . reduces investment" (77).

[52] Actually, there is much evidence that "middle-class" personal savings were higher than realized by most economists. But high interest rates channeled these savings into money-market funds and savings certificates. The standard business view was and is that high profits were required to raise the ratio of savings to personal income.

[53] In mid-1980, the Joint Economic Committee recommended that at least 50 percent of the next tax cut be designed to raise productivity. Carter's tax policy (announced in September 1980) favored large tax cuts tilted toward capital investment in the form of new schemes which would reduce the capital depreciation period. The Republican–Reagan scheme was similar, although the expected revenue loss would be much greater ("Carter's plan: reduce taxes, lure investment," *Business Week*, September 8, 1980).

[54] The author of this claim subsequently backtracked somewhat: "'Superstar' Feldstein and his little mistake," *Dollars and Sense* (December 1980).

normal mechanisms of the market. Unemployment, austerity, and a purge of the system's fat tissues, especially the heavy layer of "unreal" popular expectations created by "irresponsible" and "weak" politicians and bureaucrats would "create a new prosperity" (in Reagan's words).[55] Government policy would be brought into line with these views on the causes and consequences of the economic crisis; the "new" supply-side economics was transparently the ancient economics of *laissez-faire*.[56]

The failure of President Carter's brand of *laissez-faire* turned out to be dangerous enough to force policymakers to drop the strict monetarism adopted in 1979. The Federal Reserve Bank shifted policy focus to the control of interest rates rather than the domestic money supply itself (which many economists regarded as an obsolete concept, given the growth of uncontrollable international money movements). Britain and Canada followed suit. It became increasingly apparent to most leaders in the developed world that, in the absence of cooperative international fiscal and monetary policies, economic expansion in the USA would be essential to pull the rest of the world out of the 1981–82 recession. Subsequently, Reagan's "military Keynesianism" and huge Federal budgetary deficits,[57] higher

[55] Even a leading social democrat such as John K. Galbraith could write that "the problem is not of knowledge but of political will": "Inflation: a presidential catechism," *New York Times Magazine* (September 1974), 90. The *Times* itself began the chorus of those who blamed the government for any and all economic problems (e.g. "It has taken economists and politicians a decade to produce the soaring inflation and plummeting recession of today. It could take years to untangle the mess": *New York Times*, December 29, 1974).

[56] A good account is Lester Thurow, *Dangerous Currents: The State of Economics* (New York, 1983). "Modernized" neo-classical economics include the growing fad of "rational expectations" theory.

[57] In 1980 the US national debt was $914 billion. In early 1984 the debt reached $1.6 trillion. By 1990 it was expected to reach $2.8 trillion. In that event, interest payments on the debt would be over $200 billion annually, or a tax of about $3000 per year on every US household. This "tax" would flow ultimately to holders of the public debt (investors, institutions, and others), foreign and domestic. Marx once wrote that the public debt was one lever of primitive accumulation; it may be that the debt today will become the most important lever of decadent capitalist accumulation.

levels of consumer and mortgage borrowing and business debt, as well as the economic and political weakness of organized labor, combined to bring about the "Reagan recovery" of 1983–84. Policymakers expected that economic expansion in the USA, together with high interest rates and the inflow of foreign capital,[58] hence an overvalued dollar, would boost European and Japanese exports and thus spread the recovery overseas.

However, despite increased modernization investments in 1984, few economists expected a strong and lasting period of world economic expansion. The US economy grew by 6 per-cent in 1983,[59] western European economies by only 1 percent. Modernization investments in most developed countries increased youth unemployment to record levels. The increase in European exports to the USA was offset by the drain of capital and the subsequent rise in interest rates in Europe. West Germany, among other countries, pressured the USA to devalue the dollar in order to expand capital supplies overseas. The threat of Third World loan defaults in 1983–84 also threatened the value of the dollar. Meanwhile, many economic officials and the Federal Reserve Bank warned that a continuation of the "recovery" would cause a new round of inflation and soaring interest rates. The business pages warned that the foundations of the "Reagan recovery" were in fact hurting, not helping, the revival of US and world capitalism[60] – especially small business and "family farmers", who faced unprecedented interest payments.[61] The culprits were the huge and growing

[58] Inflows of foreign capital helped to finance the Federal deficit. In 1983 foreigners financed about 15 percent of the $200 billion deficit: "Borrowing from abroad," *Dollars and Sense* (May–June 1984).

[59] One reason for the growth of US corporations between 1983 and 1984 was that two-thirds of their external financing was short-term debt – an unprecedented level.

[60] A good summary is Emma Rothschild, "The costs of Reaganism," *The New York Review*, March 15, 1984.

[61] "For the first time in history, the total amount of interest payments on farm loans had surpassed the total new farm income": Heather Bell and Eland Beatty, "Blowing away the family farmer," *The Nation*, November 3, 1984, 422.

Federal deficit; over-expansion of debt on every economic front; the overvalued dollar, which helped to cause huge deficits in the US balance of trade (which, in turn, threatened to bring about massive withdrawals of capital by foreign investors); high real interest rates; and weak economic recoveries in most of the developed countries, hence a sharp decline in imports of debt-burdened Third World countries.

The result was growing demands in business circles (which were not openly protectionist) for corporatist-type rein-dustrialization schemes – a kind of planned neo-liberalism to help the US economy reorganize itself in terms of real and potential economic "comparative advantages." The premise of these projects was that the US was increasingly interdependent in a world economy which it remained able to dominate financially and, precisely for this reason, not industrially. The implication was that the power of the big banks to go to any lengths to protect the value of the dollars which they held would have to be weakened; that more conservative regulation of banking and finance at home would be needed; and, last but not least, that the "good of the nation" would require more sacrifices of "uneconomic" communities and dreams of an equitable and just society.

Signs and Views of Political and Social Crisis

Economists were not alone in their growing worries about world crisis trends. Sociologists, political scientists, and others also found abundant evidence consistent with their definitions of social and political crisis and what some observers regarded as greater personal stresses and strains in the "age of anxiety." Some scholars linked social distress and political turmoil in the Third World to growing poverty, unemployment, and external debt. In countries such as Brazil, Argentina, and Chile, it was widely agreed that the crisis of import-substitute industrializ-ation in the early 1960s led to the imposition of right-wing and militaristic governments and a long cycle of hardship, resistance, and repression; and, with the advent of new export-oriented industrialization in the 1970s and 1980s, new but

fragile "democratic openings' in the mid-1980s. In other countries (e.g. Iran), religious fundamentalist reactions to capitalist
modernization created endless internal turmoil and external
aggression. Left-wing governments seized power in the southern
tier of Africa; armed resistance to apartheid grew inside
South Africa itself; and a fateful cycle of revolutionary and
counter-revolutionary struggles promised permanent "troubles."
Political normalization in the Philippines and some other Asian
countries, as well as most of Africa and the Middle East, proved
more elusive than ever. Bourgeois and other scholars generally
agreed that growing inequalities in the Third World and the
decline of the "middle class" and "political center" meant that a
new social base for revolution and counter-revolution was
deepening, especially in Central America. Many "experts"
continued to argue that the military held out the best hope for
"modernization" and development (others stressed the need for
"democratic paths" in the Third World). These experts were
more often than not ideologically or practically linked to the US
government's attempt to reassert its military and economic
domination in the Third World. Nearly everyone agreed that
"democratic governments" were in permanent crisis but also
that the contradictions facing "bourgeois military" regimes
were at least as extreme. Antagonisms between the USA and the
Soviet Union grew worse; Japan's economic triumphs in the
world market generally and its penetration of the Third World
in particular caused more strains between the new "industrial
wonder of the world" and its North American and West
European competitors; last but not least, the famous "Western
Alliance" was increasingly troubled and its premises were
openly questioned.[62] Yet, by 1985, the USA had regained much
of the hegemony in relation to Europe and the Third World that
it had lost during the preceding two decades.[63]

[62] For example, Helmut Schmidt, "Saving the Western Alliance," *The New
York Review*, May 31, 1984.

[63] Perry Anderson, Folker Froebel, Jürgen Heinrichs, Otto Kreye, "On
some postulates of an anti-systemic policy," paper delivered at the United
Nations University Conference on "Human and Social Development in
Europe within Interregional and Global Perspectives," Warsaw, June 4–8,
1984.

In the developed capitalist world, sociologists and political scientists agreed that new forms of social and political crisis first appeared in the mid-1960s. Political decadence in the Third World and the system of international relations was matched by what many described as a crisis of legitimacy as well as of national and international crisis management systems; a decline in the efficacy of political party systems; a shortage of capable political leadership; and a kind of anarchy within state bureaucracies. In the USA, most Americans in the 1950s seemed to be satisfied with a political system and party competition which inserted "the public into politics in ways that permitted elite patterns of action to be legitimated without too much popular interference."[64] By the end of the 1960s, Theodore Lowi could write that 'there is serious doubt about the efficacy and justice in the agencies of government, the processes of policy-making, leadership selection, and the implementation of decisions.'[65]

By the mid-1970s, the US "public" had lost more faith in politicians and the political party system itself,[66] hence were "more disconnected from the process of legitimating 'elite patterns of action' than at any time in the past two generations."[67] One survey of half a dozen polls (all of which reported public hostility to conventional politics) concluded that, although most citizens looked to the government to solve social and economic problems and "voted issues" not parties, two-fifths of those polled did not believe that it mattered who won national elections.[68] A study commissioned by *Newsday* in 1976 warned that most Americans held pessimistic views about the future (one-half of those polled under 25 years old said that the USA was "getting to be a worse place to live in"). However, the poll also indicated that many people, especially those over

[64] Ira Katznelson, "What do voters want?", *Working Papers* (Winter 1977), 92.
[65] Theodore J. Lowi, *The End of Liberalism* (New York, 1969), xii.
[66] Norman H. Nie, Sidney Verba and John Petrocik, *The Changing American Voter* (Cambridge, Mass., 1976).
[67] Katznelson, "What do voters want?"
[68] Norman C. Miller, "A pessimistic public," *Wall Street Journal*, February 2, 1976.

25 years of age, expected their personal futures to be successful and prosperous. The editors interpreted these findings to mean that people had more confidence in themselves than they did in their government and public leaders. The leaders of big business emphatically agreed. In the mid-1970s, a study by Leonard Silk and David Vogel concluded that businessmen were deeply troubled by the apparent "incompatibility" between capitalism and democracy and the "irresponsibility" of the voters and elected representatives of the people.[69]

By the mid-1980s, the privatization of life and ideologies of neo-individualism were more firmly entrenched in mainstream America, despite popular opposition to the Reagan government's foreign and domestic policy, and despite impulses toward a new "social individuality."[70] One writer openly denounced the "thoughtless" proliferation of new social and political rights and called for more social discipline and respect for the "claims of society."[71] Another investigation described middle-American society as a kind of sinkhole of "radical atomized individualism" where isolated individuals were "motivated by feelings, desires, and fears that can be easily manipulated."[72] Still another study indicated a powerful tendency on the part of many to blame individuals in power for institutional failures and economic problems. Between 1960 and 1980, public confidence in leaders of business, unions, and other institutions, as well as the state administration and Congress, fell dramatically.[73] Public opinion held that "we have a good system run by bad or inadequate people."[74] It was only

---

[69] Leonard Silk and David Vogel, *Ethics and Profits: The Crisis of Confidence in American Business* (New York, 1976).

[70] O'Connor, *Accumulation Crisis*, chapter 8.

[71] Richard E. Morgan, *Disabling America: The "Rights Industry" in Our Time* (New York, 1985).

[72] Robert N. Bellah et al., *Habits of the Heart: Individualism and Commitment in American Life* (Berkeley, Cal., 1985).

[73] Seymour Martin Lipset and William Schneider, *The Confidence Gap: Business, Labor, and Government in the Public Mind* (New York, 1981). The percentage of people who had "great confidence" in their leaders fell between 50 percent and 75 percent.

[74] Ibid., 391. The authors stress the disparity between Americans' sense of

after the "Reagan recovery" of 1983–85 that "confidence in US institutions" was partially restored.[75]

In the 1960s and 1970s voting trends paralleled statistical findings by pollsters. Fewer people identified with mainstream political parties, more people voted "independent," and split-ticket voting increased. Participation in national elections was stagnant or in decline. Political mediocrity reigned supreme in western Europe as well as in the USA. In part thanks to the "personalization" of social and political issues by the mass media, voters seemed to be less interested in political principles than in "issues" and intangible personal qualities – for example, image and the capacity to smooth over difficult problems. The consensus of mainstream scholarship was that the voting public deeply believed in a "free society" and American individualism; hence that economic, social, and other problems arose because of the personal failings of leaders rather than the systemic and social contradictions of "late" capitalist economy, society, and state.[76]

The 1960s and 1970s also ushered in new social and economic struggles and "new social movements" which were far more politically significant than opinion polls and voting behavior. General strikes and working-class protest, from Montreal to Tel Aviv, Milan to Lagos, Paris to Sidney – from the open revolts of the late 1960s and early 1970s to the West German workers' demand for a 35-hour week in 1984 and an increase in strikes in the USA in 1985 – shook capital's confidence in itself and its institutions. The same was true of autonomous struggles in the form of refusals to work at the capitalist pace of work, wildcats and industrial sabotage, and demonstrations and riots by the reserve armies of labor, especially by oppressed minorities; and direct struggles within and against state bureaucracies around issues of de-industrializ-

---

"wellbeing" and what they regard as "social disorder." The authors' goal, of course, is to "restore public confidence."

[75] According to a Gallup Poll (*San Francisco Chronicle*, July 15, 1985).

[76] The state is deeply involved in economic and social life in advanced capitalism; hence "quality leadership" in public life is in fact as well as in belief essential for the effective functioning of society.

ation, public housing, education, worker safety, public utility regulation, welfare programs, and the police apparatus. Rapid and massive worldwide proletarianization, the internationalization of capitalist production, and capital concentration and centralization "implicated" the working classes of the world in certain common purposes, however latent or implicit. The target of the struggles of the world surplus labor army was primarily the state and state economic and social policies. Struggles of employed workers were also often political; wage conflicts in the context of "incomes policies" and IMF-imposed austerity programs could be successful only at the level of national state policy. Everywhere political means to economic and social ends were exploited inside and outside of the workplace. These strong trends, which culminated in the counter-reforms and counter-revolutions of the 1980s, were explained by bourgeois political scientists in terms of "excessive democracy," "ungovernability," and the "revolution of rising expectations and entitlements."[77] Mass politics and modern party systems (it was implied) had become barriers to capitalist accumulation. The capacity of governments to impose discipline and sacrifices on their citizens, in order to achieve social and political goals which would help not hinder capital, was undermined (it was argued) by the consumer society and its stress on "private satisfaction, leisure . . . and intellectual and aesthetic self-fulfillment."[78]

Problems of social as well as political integration and stability were also part of the cultural sea changes of the 1960s and 1970s. "In the past there was a broad middle class. It was a kind of bell-shaped curve. What you see now is a pulling apart. If you're not on the escalator up, you're being pulled down."[79]

[77] The classic text is Michael Crozier, Samuel Huntington, and Joji Watanuki, *The Crisis of Democracy: Report on the Governability of Democracies to the Trilateral Commission* (New York, 1975).

[78] Ibid., 7.

[79] Peter Morrison, Director of Population Research, Rand Corporation, quoted in *San Francisco Examiner*, July 22, 1984. If a "middle-class family" is defined as a married couple (with or without children) with an annual income of between $15,000 and $35,000 yearly, with the husband as the sole wage

The informality of this account belies the social dangers of the ominous "decline of the middle class" (mentioned above), which foreshadowed rising divorce rates, the "feminization of poverty," increased violence against women and children, revived racism and fascistic tendencies (especially in western Europe), a new and dangerous unquestioning patriotism, and a kind of generalized "lack of caring." These and other signs of capitalist social disintegration were only partly checked by, on the one hand, a struggling local communalism and, on the other, a runaway individual success ethic by the new well-to-do, who defended modern individualism as the real source of social solidarity.

Social disintegration and social crisis tendencies created not only popular distrust and anger, fear and envy, but also widespread theorizing within mainstream sociology and social psychology. Three kinds of explanations of the "social problem" appeared in academic and mass-media discussions and debates. The first drew causal arrows between the growth of low-paid service jobs, unemployment in the older industries, and the polarization of income distribution, on the one side, and the decay of the patriarchal family system, the "crisis of authority," and so on, on the other. The second drew attention to the breakdown of traditional institutional ties within the workplace, family, and religious and other institutions, together with the incapacity of the bureaucratic state and impersonal corporation to produce new values and meanings which could underwrite new forms of social solidarity. This kind of explanation gave theoretical primacy not to economic trends themselves but to the growth of new "institutional imperatives" within large-scale capitalist organizations and the state. The third explanation stressed the rise of consumerism and the obsession with "personal growth" and the "cult of the self."

---

earner, recent census data show that the percentage of these households declined and the proportion of low- and high-income households increased. In 1970, 48 per cent of households were middle-income; in 1982, only 39.5 percent. The proportion of low-income households rose from 33.5 percent to 37.4 percent and high-income households increased from 18.5 percent to 22 percent.

Academic Panglossians celebrated new opportunities for individual self-expression and development in the context of what they regarded as the "end of scarcity" and the decline of "inner-directed" traditions.[80] Pollsters argued that the USA remains a "strong, progress-oriented land" populated by an optimistic people.[81] However, pessimists called attention to the adverse effects of the cult of "self" on social integration in general and public life in particular.[82] These scholars regarded modern narcissism as the long shadow of traditional bourgeois individuality which, however, conflicted with normative structures in the capitalist workplace and diminished individual capacities to adapt to changing roles and structures associated with massive economic and social change. In this darker view, the fetishism of "personality" and the associated weakening of traditional institutions such as the family and church caused individuals to become increasingly dependent on state institutions, which displaced contradictions between new economic imperatives and cultural norms into the public bureaucracies. Or they created a desperate need by many people to compensate for the "lost order" of tradition by joining totalitarian religious, political, and other sects, meanwhile developing dangerously rigid character structures (more so even than the traditional armor-plated bourgeois personality). According to Christopher

---

[80] David Riesman (*The Lonely Crowd: A Study of the Changing American Character* (New Haven, Conn., 1960)) was the most important forerunner of this tradition and may be regarded as a "qualified optimist." A more unabashed optimist was Erik Erikson (*Childhood and Society* (New York, 1963)). Others included Norman O. Brown, Theodore Roszak, and Charles Reich. All of these writers grounded their arguments partly or wholly in the "end of scarcity" premise. Riesman later called attention to the subversive effects of consumerism on the work ethic and productivity, in this way critiquing his own "end of scarcity" thesis. An excellent review of this issue is Robert Ehrlich, "Review," Daniel Yankelovich, *New Rules for Self-Fulfillment in a World Turned Upside Down* (New York, 1981), *Telos*, 50 (Winter 1981–82). Yankelovich is the latest "optimist."

[81] "Interview with Ben Wattenberg," *San Francisco Chronicle*, January 2, 1985.

[82] Daniel Bell, *The Cultural Crisis of Capitalism* (New York, 1976); Christopher Lasch, *The Culture of Narcissism: American Life in an Age of Diminishing Expectations* (New York, 1978).

Lasch, US society was increasingly made up of emotionally manipulative individuals with little self-esteem and constant feelings of emptiness which (in a variation of this thesis) leads to a "flight from identity" and "disengagement and emotional numbness."[83] This account is certainly consistent with the facts of modern manic-depression and social anxiety – in short, a society of omnipotent/helpless children with weak egos and socially distorted superegos whose "political drift to the right" in the 1980s was all but preordained.

Conclusion

This brief survey of crisis trends and bourgeois crisis theories suggests that the fragmentation of academic social science fatally weakens its ability to develop a "unified field theory" of the modern crisis of capitalism. Sociologists and political scientists "explain" such problems as weak social motivations, political apathy, and political crisis wholly or partly in terms of economic trends.[84] Economists "explain" economic crisis tendencies wholly or partly in terms of the effects of the politicization of the economy on motivations and incentives. "Independent variables" in one field are thus "dependent variables" in other fields. Political scientists and sociologists take for granted what economists regard as problematic; economists accept in a matter-of-fact way crisis trends which other social scientists see as deep puzzles. Bourgeois social science is thus a theoretical house of cards which explains little or nothing. Economy, society, and the state are not seen as a "concrete totality" but as separate spheres of social action with their own more or less autonomous rules or "laws of motion."

[83] Herbert Hendin, *The Age of Sensation: A Psychoanalytical Study of the Youth of the Seventies* (New York, 1975).

[84] For example, "political crisis" is often defined as periods when there occurs a major realignment of electoral groupings which is typically regarded as wholly or partially determined by economic factors (e.g. Thomas Ferguson and Joel Rogers (eds), *The Hidden Election: Politics and Economics in the 1980 Presidential Campaign* (New York, 1981), *passim*.

In this way, social science reproduces in thought the appearance of a separate capitalist economy, social life, and politics. No possibilitiy of an imminent critique exists. There is only a certain moralizing with which the urgings, pontifications, implorings, and supplications of politicians and celebrities inundate mass consciousness to the point of total boredom. In sum, today are celebrated nineteenth-century economic incentives, social goals, and political processes which have long ago self-destructed and metamorphosed into the rawest kind of ideologies.

This is why bourgeois crisis theories are in the last analysis irrelevant at best and reactionary at worst. The academic echoes of the roar of international big capital reverberate through the ideological canyons of a terribly feared future. They call for a return to a mythical past of progress and prosperity; the present is not regarded as history in the making but rather history as a reified past. The call to arms is an entreatment simultaneously to work and save *and* borrow and consume; to stay home with the family *and* leave home to fill the ranks of the exploding service economy; to accept uncritically the new international economy and division of labor *and* at the same time "rebuild America;" defend liberty against state regulation and encroachment *and* bow before the imperatives of national security and state-imposed order,[85] *ad nauseam*. Bourgeois theory is thus inevitably not part of the solution to the modern crisis but rather a central problem of late capitalist society.[86]

[85] The attacks on the Bill of Rights by the Supreme Court in 1983–84 tempt many to "characterize the Court's decisions as 'conservative,' [but] it is far more accurate to describe them as 'statist'": Burt Neuborne and Charles Sims, "Americans are far less free today than they were a year ago," *Civil Liberties* (Summer 1984), 12.

[86] It is ironic that some bourgeois social scientists themselves recognize the truth of this proposition. Keynesian and neo-Keynesian economists have been scapegoated for economic failures by the neo-liberals; political scientists who have taught that politics is the rational pursuit of self-interest have been scapegoated for political failures by the traditionalists (e.g. Morris Janowitz, *The Reconstruction of Patriotism: Education for Civic Consciousness* (Chicago, 1984)).

2

Economic Crisis Theory

Introduction

The idea of "crisis" is at the heart of all serious discussions of the modern world. "Few will doubt that the crisis which engulfed the twentieth century is a genuine crisis . . . the idea of crisis is penetrating the most varied fields of human activities."[1] This is especially true in the field of Marxist political economy. The social and economic crises beginning in the late 1960s have stimulated a vigorous revival of Marxist theories of recession and inflation, unemployment, poverty, and other crisis signs and symptoms. The purpose of this revival is to explain the economic crisis in ways which help to empower working-class and social movements, and independence movements in the Third World, and to strengthen the left's capacity to survive and struggle on the political and ideological terrain of the 1980s.

So far, attempts to renew and renovate Marxist crisis theory have had little political success. One reason is that Marxism does not yet have close connections with "new social movements," nor still less with the counter-cultures of the 1980s. Another is that Marxism has become increasingly politically suspect at a time when, ironically, it has become a respectable academic discipline. These are related to the fact that the Marxist revival has respected "time-honored" and "time-

[1] Gerhard Masur, "Crisis in history," *Dictionary of the History of Ideas*, vol. I (New York, 1968), 595.

worn" classical traditions. While there are some notable exceptions which we will encounter during our theoretical journey,
neo-orthodox Marxism does not grasp the present economic
crisis as new in the sense of demanding new conceptual tools
and methods. Whatever the particular explanations of the
present crisis offered by neo-orthodox Marxists, most if not all
theories remain "economic determinist."[2] The same can be said
of most varieties of revisionist Marxism, including the "Keynesian Marxists," who pioneered theories of monopoly capitalism and permanent economic stagnation but whose work is
firmly lodged within the broad tradition of Marxist political
economy.[3]

Marx's classical theory of economic crisis is that "the contradiction, specific to capitalism, between exchange-value and
use-value production"[4] means that capital periodically creates
its own "internal barriers" to economic expansion, and
therefore that "the limit of capital is capital itself." This theory
is interpreted by most Marxists today in terms of traditional

[2] For example, Paul Mattick, *Marx and Keynes: The Limits of the Mixed
Economy* (Boston, Mass., 1969); *Economics, Politics, and the Age of Inflation*
(White Plains, NY, 1978); *Economic Crisis and Crisis Theory* (London,
1981). Mattick is widely respected as one of the best neo-orthodox theorists in
the English-speaking world. His acknowledged strengths are his encyclopedic
knowledge of the history of crisis theory and his rigorous defense of Marxist
economic orthodoxy.

[3] For example, Michael Kalecki, *Theory of Economic Dynamics* (New
York, 1965) and *The Last Phase in the Transformation of Capitalism* (New
York, 1972); Paul A. Baran and Paul M. Sweezy, *Monopoly Capital: An
Essay on the American Economic and Social Order* (New York, 1966); Harry
Magdoff and Paul M. Sweezy, *The End of Prosperity: The American
Economy in the 1970s* (New York, 1977). Kalecki first synthesized Keynesian
and Marxian theory in the context of a capitalist economy with unused
capacity and less than full employment. Kalecki also developed a theory of
stagnation based on the idea that monopolies slow down the rate of
introduction of new innovations to protect the value of their capital, and that
fewer investment outlets appear in the monopoly stage of capitalism for other
reasons. The acknowledged strength of Baran, Sweezy, and Magdoff's work
includes their insistence on detailed empirical analyses and the importance of
"exterior, historical circumstances," especially wars and technical innovations, as engines of capitalist accumulation.

[4] Mattick, *Economic Crisis and Crisis Theory*, 6.

theories of overproduction of capital and/or the tendency of the profit rate to fall.[5] These approaches to crisis theory will be expounded below. They doubtless made good sense before the development of the bureaucratic state, the "administered society," "political capitalism," the "social factory," contemporary labor and social movements, and Third World struggles. In the present epoch, however, classical theories of economic crisis need modification or revision, even though most theorists today are keenly aware of some of the most important new trends in capitalism today, especially the fact that the present crisis "is a crisis of the capitalist world system and no more a crisis of only this or that capitalist nation,"[6] hence the need to broaden the approach of traditional crisis theory. The enormous expansion of credit on a world scale – which suppresses deep economic depression at the cost of huge state budgetary deficits and/or inflation and a resulting international "debt crisis" – is one new trend.[7] Another is the internationalization of capitalist production, which immensely complicates the analysis of short- and long-run crisis tendencies as well as sectoral and/or regional crises associated with the process of uneven and combined development of capital.[8] Still another is the growth of finance capital and monopoly capital and new roles for the political system and state bureaucracy in the process of capitalist accumulation, especially with regard to

[5] For example, Ernest Mandel, *Late Capitalism* (London, 1975).

[6] Elmar Altvater, "The double character of the current crisis of the capitalist world system," *Socialism in the World*, 8, 42 (1984), 3.

[7] Marx was the first to theorize that an independent credit system is inherent in capitalism, and that credit expansion may function to prevent crises, but "at the price of internalizing the contradictions within itself. Massive concentration of financial power, accompanied by the machinations of finance capital, can as easily destabilize as stabilize capitalism": David Harvey, *The Limits to Capital* (Oxford, 1982), xvi. What is new today is the massive increase in consumer and mortgage debt, Federal government deficits, and the international "debt crisis" which has been thoroughly politicized through International Monetary Fund austerity programs.

[8] For example, Folker Froebel, Jürgen Heinrichs, and Otto Kreye, *The New International Division of Labour* (Cambridge, 1980); Stephen Herbert Hymer, *The Multinational Corporation: A Radical Approach* (Cambridge, 1979).

capital restructuring,[9] the modernization of old zones of heavy industry, and the development of high technology associated with the internationalization of production, militarism, and economic crisis itself. Furthermore, many contemporary Marxists have tried to fit classical theories of capital overproduction and/or the falling profit rate into a broader social and political framework and have pioneered the concept of an "accumulation model." Yet, beyond a keen recognition of these trends and the development of valuable broader concepts of "crisis," which include social and political as well as economic structural changes and transformations, the revival of Marxist orthodoxy offers little theoretical novelty or (so far) political utility.[10]

However, because most Marxist crisis theory today is a "revival" and "renewal" of classical traditions, and because modern labor movements remain influenced by these traditions (while "new social movements" continue to function in a theoretical vacuum), it is worthwhile to review and evaluate the main premises and arguments of neo-orthodox crisis theory. This is the basic purpose of this chapter. A secondary purpose is to assess the strengths and weaknesses of that branch of Marxist crisis theory which takes as its point of departure the class struggle between capital and labor.[11] While the neo-orthodox "systems" theory of crisis has its intellectual origins in the critical and scientific tradition of the Enlightenment, "class struggle" theory springs from anti-Enlightenment, Romantic,

---

[9] For example, "The concept of restructuring of capital helps us to overcome the old dichotomy between economic and political analysis by specifying capital accumulation and value movements within the context of the economic class relations and class political constellations which obstruct or facilitate such transformations. The related concept [of class] strategies helps to free the concept of capital restructuring from any residual essentialism or economic functionalism": Hugh Mosley, "Capital and the state: West German neo-orthodox state theory," *Review of Radical Political Economics* (*RRPE*), 14, 1 (Spring, 1982).

[10] Eclectic works (for example, Manuel Castells, *The Economic Crisis and American Society* (Princeton, NJ, 1980)) which combine orthodox Marxist economics with neo-Marxist social theory are partial exceptions.

[11] For example, Harry Cleaver and Peter Bell, "Marx's crisis theory as a theory of class relations," *Research in Political Economy*, 5 (1982); Toni Negri, *Marx Beyond Marx* (South Hadley, Mass., 1984).

and modernist thought and is the main alternative to classical or "objectivist" Marxism. "Class struggle" theorists define crisis in terms not of "internal barriers" to capitalist accumulation but of an "external barrier," the working class itself.[12] Their focus is the condition of availability of disciplined wage labor, or capital's political and ideological capacity to impose wage labor on the working class.[13] Put another way, its focus is the theory of crisis as a theory of capital and the theory of surplus value as a theory of revolution.[14] The main premise is that "the *fundamental cause of the crisis [lies] in the relation between*

[12] Michael Lebowitz uses the terms "specific" and "general" barriers to capitalist accumulation, the first referring to what is inherent in the capitalist model of production, the second to what exists in any mode of production but which assumes specifically capitalist forms ("The general and the specific in Marx's theory of crisis," *Studies in Political Economy*, 7 (Winter 1982)). Lebowitz includes as "general" barriers the supply of labor and the availability of land and natural resources. As for the former, in his path-breaking article, Lebowitz does not distinguish between the supply of labor *per se* and the supply of disciplined *wage* laborers. As for the availability of natural resources, Lebowitz does not distinguish between "natural" shortages and shortages politically created by the ecological movement. Marx discussed the former "external" or "general" barrier under the general rubric of ground rent, and the way that ground rent drains industrial profits, hence the way in which this "external" barrier takes specifically capitalist forms. The effects of the political struggles of the ecology movement on costs of capital, turnover time of capital, profit movement on costs of capital, turnover time of capital, profit rate, etc., have received short shrift by nearly all Marxist political economists. The same is true of the effects of the disruption of ecological balances on costs, prices, and profits. I am working on these issues in a planned book called *Capital and the Crisis of Nature*.

[13] See also Harry Cleaver, "Preface," *Reading Capital Politically* (Austin, Texas, 1979). This "sociological" approach to crisis theory has received empirical support in a new historical study based on the idea of "long waves" of capitalist expansion and contraction: Ernesto Screpanti, "Long cycles in strike activity: an empirical investigation," Universita degli Studi di Trento, Dipartimento di Economia, MS (1985).

Also in the family of "class struggle" approaches is "profit squeeze" theory. See Andrew Glyn and Bob Sutcliffe, *Capitalism in Crisis* (New York, 1972); Raford Boddy and James Crotty, "Class conflict and macro-policy: the political business cycle," *RRPE*, 7, 1 (1975). In this perspective, labor's strength and the drying up of the reserve army of labor were the source of declining profits in the 1960s.

[14] Negri, *Marx Beyond Marx, passim.*

necessary and surplus labor, that is in the relation between the
constitutive parts of the working day and in the class relation
which constitutes it."[15] The main conclusion is that "only the
freedom of necessary labor, the creativity of labor applied to
itself, its force both creative and destructive, constitutes the real
limit of capital and the manifold, recurrent causes of its
crisis."[16] This bold view challenges neo-orthodox systems
theory with a social theory of economic crisis. Its fatal flaw is
that it tends to collapse the categories of crisis and class struggle
into the single concept of "exploitation."[17] This "black hole"
treatment of economy, society, and politics neglects the cultural
and ideological conditions of capitalist reproduction and their
relationship to the causes and consequences of economic crisis
and class struggle. No institutional or cultural mediations mar
the bold simplicity of this approach, which politically has led to
dead ends.

Neo-Orthodox Economic Crisis Theory

"Crisis" comes from the Greek word meaning "to separate or
divide" and "to sift, to decide," signifying the idea of "discrimi-
nation or decision."[18] In ancient Greece, crises were "moments
of truth when the significance of men and events were brought

---

[15] Ibid., 72.

[16] Ibid., 10. In Cleaver and Bell's words, "For workers the most important
thing about capitalist crisis is that it is, for the most part, the consequences of
their struggles. The rupture of accumulation by struggle is a moment of
conquest" ("Marx's crisis theory as a theory of class relations," 258). Again,
"the working class struggle *against* work is the source of the crisis"
(*Zerowork*, 1 (December, 1975), 5).

[17] The argument that "class struggle" crisis theory fails to locate and
ground worker struggles within the law of value generally, and the tendency of
the profit rate to fall in particular, is made in Ben Fine and Laurence Harris,
"State expenditures in advanced capitalism: a critique," *New Left Review*
(July–August 1976). The argument that the contemporary crisis is a crisis of
productivity (as "class struggle" theorists claim) is attacked in "Productivity
slowdown: a false alarm," *Monthly Review* (June, 1979), 1.

[18] Randolph Stern, "Historians and crisis," *Past and Present*, 52 (August
1970).

to light." Another meaning was the "turning point" of an illness "in which it is decided whether or not the [individual] organisms' self-healing powers are sufficient for recovery."[19]

In economic theory, "crisis" was used in the "objectivist" sense in the late seventeenth century to refer to conditions of general market disequilibria.[20] By the early nineteenth century, the word was widely employed to contrast "pathological" situations with more normal times. While the most perceptive of all the classical political economists, Simonde de Sismondi, theorized that crises were inherent features of industrial capitalism, economic hard times in ancient society and feudalism, as well as in early modern Europe, were universally regarded as pathological in that they arose from "external" causes, especially bad harvests and the politics of dearth.[21] Or they were viewed as merchant-capitalist and financial "excesses," "panics" generated by wars and political forces and/or financial speculation external to material production, hence not "normal" or regular events in economic life. Or crises were understood (as Hegel did) as what may be called "sectoral crises" – the decline of particular industries or branches of production owing to changes in conditions of demand or the emergence of low-cost competition in other regions or countries – processes which remain highly relevant to modern economic conditions.

Marx himself spoke of early "financial crises of the absolute monarchy"[22] which were political and therefore highly con-

---

[19] Jürgen Habermas, *Legitimation Crisis* (Boston, Mass., 1975), 1. In Stern's words, crises "occur in diseases whenever the disease increases in intensity or goes away or changes into another disease or ends altogether." In Melvin Rader's words, "Hippocrates introduced the term 'crisis' to characterize the turning point in a disease when death or recovery hangs in the balance": *Marx's Interpretation of History* (New York, 1979), 187.

[20] Sieur de Boisguillebert (1646–1714): Guy Routh, *The Origins of Economic Ideas* (New York, 1977), 57–9.

[21] In ancient society, "ups and downs in production were always attributable to natural catastrophes or political troubles, not to cyclical crises . . . 'credit crises' turn out to have had the same roots": Moses I. Finley, *The Ancient Economy* (Berkeley, Cal., 1973), 142.

[22] Karl Marx and Frederick Engels, *Collected Works*, vol. 6 (New York, 1976), 320.

junctural in origin. Other writers considered the English crises of 1816 and 1825 also as conjunctural – "irregular events due to external factors (mainly wars) and explained by disturbances in the functioning of the money and banking systems."[23] By 1843–44, however, Engels had sketched a theory of crisis in the *Outline of a Critique of Political Economy* which underscored the recurrence of "trade cycles" based on "unregulated production," which he explained in "simple terms of supply and demand."[24] In the *Communist Manisfesto*, published in 1848, Marx and Engels had essentially the same theory, with the exception that crises were seen as originating in the contradiction between the development of the "productive forces" and the "narrow" conditions of bourgeois society.[25] By the late 1850s, some writers had developed a "clear and consistent view of economic crises considered in the dimension of historic time: crises were rooted in the functioning of economic life: [they were] cyclical movements, appearing with a certain regularity."[26] As for Marx himself, "we cannot find an investigation into cycles in [his] crises theory . . . but he did operate with this concept inasmuch as he connected the crises with the ten year renewal, on the average, of production equipment. Nevertheless, Marx had not elaborated the main features of the cycle."[27]

On the basis of interpretations of Marx's theoretical work in *Capital*, published in 1867, five generations of Marxist political

[23] E. Kemenes, *Cyclical and Secular Changes in the World Economy, Trends in World Economy* (Budapest, 1981), 8.

[24] Cleaver and Bell, "Marx's crisis theory as a theory of class relations," 196–8.

There is no dearth of modern writers who explain the modern crisis in terms of the "overall, anarchistic situation of global production" and "cut-throat competition" (Albert Bergesen, "Crisis in the world system: an introduction," in Bergesen (ed.), *Crisis in the World-System* (Beverly Hills, Cal., 1983), 11).

[25] Cleaver and Bell, "Marx's crisis theory as a theory of class relations," 202, quoting Marx.

[26] The author of this particular "clear and consistent view" was Lord Overstone (*Tracts and Other Publications on Metallic and Paper Currency* (London, 1858), in Kemenes, *Cyclical and Secular Changes in World Economy* 9).

[27] Ibid.

economists, including neo-orthodox Marxists today, came to define "crisis" as an interruption in the accumulation of capital which is "inevitable" in the sense that the capitalist mode of production develops the productive forces without limit, while attempting in a variety of ways to preserve their present value.[28] Marx himself defined crises as "violent eruptions" which "are always but forcible solutions of the existing contradictions . . . which for a time restore the disturbed equilibrium."[29] In the words of one modern political economist, "what was significant about a crisis is that it revealed the existence of a barrier to capital. Given the essential nature of capital as self-expanding value, a crisis was a manifestation of an inherent check on its growth – a moment in which capital has come against barriers which thwart its impulse."[30] Crises are thus regarded as neither pathological nor accidental, nor as the result of disequilibria between supply and demand, but rather as "objective" processes of economic-system disruption (and, as we shall see, economic restructuring). Marx and his orthodox followers, no matter what specific interpretations the latter made of the seemingly contradictory passages in *Capital* on the origins and functions of economic crisis,[31] held that crises were normal features of capitalist development. The rise of industrial capital and the growing importance of fixed capital and credit money generated "violent eruptions" within the process of accumulation and economic hard times as a matter of course.

It is clear from this brief account that, in orthodox and neo-orthodox Marxist theory, "capital" is regarded as having a life of its own, a reified existence, and "decides" its own "turning points" or critical movements of crisis (and, subsequently, economic depression and recovery). Human beings do

[28] Ben Fine, *Marx's Capital* (London, 1975), 51.
[29] Karl Marx, *Capital*, III, 249. All references to *Capital* are to the International Publishers (New York) 1967 edition.
[30] Lebowitz, "The general and the specific in Marx's theory of crisis," 6.
[31] The best modern account of the many variations of Marxist crisis theory developed within the orthodox tradition is Mattick, *Economic Crisis and Crisis Theory*, chapter 3. This book is also invaluable as an account of Marx's own crisis theories found in *Capital*.

not willfully produce economic crises, nor can human intervention within the dominant capitalist relations of production
prevent crises, although crises may be postponed or displaced
by political means.[32] Human beings, in fact, are regarded as
mere personifications of the categories of capital – not exchange
relations alone, as in bourgeois crisis theory, but as relations of
production, circulation, competition, credit, and so on, i.e. the
reproduction process of capital as a whole. This organismic and
objectivistic concept of "crisis" is clearly analogous to the use of
the word in medical science. Engels himself referred to
economic crisis in medical terms. "The course of the social
disease from which England is suffering is the same as the
course of a physical disease; it develops according to certain
laws, has its own crisis, the last and most violent of which
determines the fate of the patient."[33] In his neo-Marxist work
on crisis theory, Jürgen Habermas expands on this metaphor
with his view that the critical moment appears as something
"objective" or external, hence

the crisis cannot be separated from the viewpoint of the one who is
undergoing it – during an illness the patient experiences his powerlessness *vis à vis* the objectivity of his illness only because he is a subject
condemned to passivity and temporarily deprived of the possibility of
being a subject in full possession of his power ... we therefore
associate with crises the idea of an objective force that deprives a
subject of some part of his normal sovereignty.[34]

In neo-orthodox marxist theory, the "subject" is capital
itself, the "valorization" process or process of capitalist wealth
production and accumulation, which is deprived of its "normal
sovereignty" by the "objective" force of economic crises. Capital defined as the social relationships of production and
accumulation loses full possession of its powers when too many
and/or too large and/or too prolonged ruptures occur within

[32] For example, James O'Connor, *The Fiscal Crisis of the State* (New York,
1973), chapters 1 and 2.
[33] Marx and Engels, *Collected Works*, vol. 4, 419.
[34] Habermas, *Legitimation Crisis*, 1.

and between the money, productive, and commodity circuits of capital. Capital's ordeal ends temporarily with the restoration of its "sovereignty" through the re-establishment of the unity between production and circulation and the process of capital restructuring. Crisis is thus a turning point in the process of material production and distribution in which it is decided whether the system's "self-healing powers" are sufficient for recovery and renewal of capital accumulation. "Crises are 'creative ruptures' in the continuity of the reproduction of social relationships which lead to their restructuring in new forms."[35] In the tradition of "class struggle" crisis theory, "restructuring social relationships" are described much more forcefully: "As the most fundamental contradiction of capitalism is between the classes, so the most fundamental role of crisis-as-solution is restoring the balance of class forces such that capital can resume its growth, i.e., growth in its control of the working class and society."[36]

No single or dominant concept *or* theory of crisis may be found in Marx's own works. With regard to crisis theory, some of Marx's followers have argued that he held to an approach focused on over production of capital; others maintain that his real position centered on the (admittedly sketchy) theory of the tendency of the falling profit rate. A few have concentrated on disproportionalities between different branches of the economy as the source of economic crisis. Many have insisted that changes brought about by the development of "monopoly capitalism" and "state monopoly capitalism" in relation to both short- and long-run economic movements require a different approach to crisis theory. With regard to the concept of crisis itself, the idea of "capitalist breakdown" has coexisted uneasily with the classical concept of the business cycle and sectoral crises associated with the uneven development of

---

[35] Mike Davis, "'Fordism' in crisis: a review of Michael Aglietta's *Regulation et crises: l'experience des États-Unis*," *Review*, 2, 2 (Fall 1978), 212. The English edition of Aglietta's book is *A Theory of Capitalist Regulation, the US Experience* (London, 1979).

[36] Cleaver and Bell, "Marx's crisis theory as a theory of class relations," 257.

capital, on the one hand, and more contemporary theories of long-run structural crises, "long waves" of economic activity, and economic stagnation and "stagflation," on the other. As we know, Marx's own view of the origins of crisis was based on his theory of the contradiction between capitalist forces and relations of production.[37] Yet it has been argued persuasively that Marx "explicitly rejects any monocausal explanation" and, it may be added, concept "of crisis, insisting that they are a combination of *all* the contradictions of the capitalist mode of production."[38]

At the risk of oversimplifying a complex issue, it can be said that neo-orthodox Marxists have identified three kinds of crisis, which have been explained in whole or in part differently by different theorists. The first are periodic crises associated with the capitalist business cycle and cyclical movements of the rate of profit. This is the kind of "crisis" which commanded Marx and Engels's attention in the late 1840s.[39] It remains a centerpiece of neo-orthodox Marxist thought in the late twentieth century.[40] However, it has been modified by the theory of the "political business cycle," which explains recessions and recoveries partly in terms of political forces.[41] It has also been challenged by theories of monopoly capitalism, which maintain that big capital "manipulates the prices of its products periodi-

---

[37] "This antagonism between modern industry and science, on the one hand, and modern misery and dissolution, on the other, this antagonism between the productive powers and the social relations of our epoch, is a fact, palpable, overwhelming, and not to be controverted" (quoted in Rader, *Marx's Interpretation of History*, 197).

[38] Ernest Mandel, "The industrial cycle in late capitalism," *New Left Review*, 90 (March–April 1975), 3.

[39] Marx and Engels, *Collected Works*, vol. 6, 347, 462.

[40] "The cyclical movement of capitalist production undoubtedly finds its clearest expression in the cyclical movement of the rate of profit, which after all sums up the contradictory development of all the moments of the process of production and reproduction" (Mandel, "The industrial cycle in late capitalism").

[41] For example, M. Kalecki, "Political aspects of full employment," in M. Kalecki, *The Last Phase in the Transformation of Capitalism* (New York, 1972): Boddy and Crotty, "Class conflict and macro-policy: the political business cycle."

cally to secure high fixed profits at any phase in the individual business cycle," thus helping to transform short-term recessions into long-term economic stagnation.[42] However, in the extreme neo-orthodox view, all capitalist crises are cyclical crises, and this is exemplified by one Marxist economist's reproach that "all theories of long-run crises are incorrect . . . there are no long-run downturns or final automatic collapses of capitalism."[43]

The second concept of crisis identified by neo-orthodox Marxists is precisely "long-run downturns" (if not "final automatic collapses") or "structural crisis" which is usually analyzed in terms of an "accumulation model." The accumulation model normally rests on the theory of overproduction of capital or the theory of the falling profit rate, and may or may not incorporate a theory of "long waves" of economic activity.[44] The strictly economistic approach to structural crisis explains long-run declines in the profit rate in terms of the rising organic composition of capital (see the next section), while interpreting cyclical movements in the rate of profit in terms of the uneven development of the capital- and consumer-goods sectors of the economy (Departments I and II, respectively).[45] More social-theoretical and structural approaches employ the idea of the accumulation model, according to which over a period of decades the capitalist relations of production, as well as conditions of social reproduction generally, adjust in the

---

[42] Seiichi Nagashima, "Business cycles under state monopoly capitalism," *Kanto Gakuin University Economic Review*, 2 (1980), 35. This theme was developed in Joseph Steindl, *Maturity and Stagnation in American Capitalism* (New York, 1976), and Baron and Sweezy, *Monopoly Capital*. The latter work argues that fixed prices and increasingly lower costs tend to widen profit margins.

[43] Howard Sherman, "Inflation, unemployment, and the contemporary business cycle," *Socialist Review*, 44 (9,2) (March–April 1979), 75. This view has some precedent in the writings of Marx himself, who stated that "permanent crises do not exist": *Theories of Surplus Value*, part 2 (New York, 1954), 373.

[44] Bergesen, "Crisis in the world-system: an introduction"; Ernest Mandel, *Long Waves of Capitalist Development* (Cambridge, 1980); T. Hopkins and I. Wallerstein (eds), *Processes of the World-System* (Beverly Hills, Cal., 1980).

[45] Mandel, "The industrial cycle in late capitalism," 4.

course of social struggles, changes in social and political institutions, and ideological twists and turns "to the requirements of the developing productive forces."[46] In this view, expansive periods of capitalist development occur within the framework of favorable structures of class and institutional relationships, as well as particular nurturing ideologies. "The framework can be said to form a specific accumulation model," Jens Hoff writes.

The relationship between the accumulation model and a structural crisis is then explained by pointing out how the structural framework of the accumulation model develops [in an] increasingly contradictory [way], and how, because of this, the accumulation model turns into a structural crisis. Structural crises can therefore be viewed as periods in the history of capitalist development when one accumulation model is substituted for another, i.e., when some structures deteriorate and others are built.[47]

One sophisticated example of this approach is Michel Aglietta's, which introduces the concept of "regulation," or "the overall unification and articulation of specific structural forms into a complex social formation . . . 'regulation' encompasses all the constraints acting upon the accumulation of capital at a particular phase of development."[48] This approach is consistent

[46] Samir Amin, "Toward a structural crisis of world capitalism," *Socialist Revolution*, 23 (5, 11) (April 1975), 9.
"Every phase of expansion is characterized by a particular accumulation model: a type of propelling industry, specific forms of competition, and a definite kind of firm. Each phase corresponds to a certain stage of geographic expansion of the capitalist system, to a particular organization of international specialization, more specifically to a functional division between the center and periphery, and finally, to a certain balance (or imbalance) among the nation-states at the center. . . . Every structural crisis constitutes a phase of 'maladjustments and readjustments' (an apt expression used by André Gundar Frank), in the transition from one accumulation model to another. Crisis means that growth is slowed, and that the class struggle intensifies" (ibid., 10).
See also Samir Amin, Giovanni Arrighi, and André Gundar Frank, *Dynamics of Global Crisis* (New York, 1982).
[47] Letter to the author, November 20, 1980.
[48] Davis, "'Fordism' in crisis," 212.

with Elmar Altvater's "distinction between *small* and *great* crises. Small crises may be called those crises which only require adaptive processes *within* the given form of social reproduction. Great crises . . . are *breaks* of more or less important parts of *of the formal structure* of social reproduction."[49] This approach is also consistent with Eric Hobsbawm's definition of "crises of capitalism" as the "rather lengthy periods of trouble, between 1815 and 1848, between 1873 and 1896, and between 1917 and 1948,"[50] a periodization which in part parallels Samir Amin's "periods of structural crisis: 1840–1850, 1870–1890, 1914–1948."[51] The accumulation model is also consistent with the concept of crisis defined by "world system" sociologists, namely, as a rupture or "disarticulation" between the development of the world division of labor and the relative power of nation-states. There is a resemblance between this approach and the work of those who interpret the present "international economic disorder" in terms of the decline of the political economic hegemony of the USA.[52] Robert Heilbroner's view that crises are "crucial junctures" which bring about "changes in seismic magnitude" also corresponds roughly with the accumulation model thesis.[53] Finally, this view is akin to the work of André Gundar Frank, Ernest Mandel, and others who have argued that modern capitalism entered into a structural crisis in the 1960s, one which cannot be resolved by policies aiming to increase profit rates alone, but which requires thoroughgoing changes in post-war institutions which have ceased to be useful to capital.[54]

The difference between the concept of crisis as periodic economic fluctuations and structural crisis is that the latter

[49] Altvater, "The double character of the current crisis of the capitalist world system," 9–10.

[50] Eric Hobsbawm, "The crisis of capitalism in historical perspective," *Socialist Review*, 30 (6, 4) (October–December 1976), 79.

[51] Amin, "Toward a structural crisis of world capitalism."

[52] Fred Block, *The Origins of the International Economic Disorder* (Berkeley, Cal., 1977).

[53] Robert Heilbroner, *Beyond Boom and Crash* (New York, 1978).

[54] André Gundar Frank, *Crisis: In the World Economy* (New York, 1980).

refers to long-term conjunctures and multiple contradictions in economic, political, and social life. The bridge between these two meanings of crisis erected in the accounts of the modern accumulation crisis by Frank, Mandel, and others is that the structural contradictions of capitalism both cause and are caused by what they regard as the increasingly short-lived and shallow cyclical economic recoveries and the deeper and longer-lasting recessions since the early 1970s.

The final concept of crisis found in the literature of neo-orthodox Marxist theory is sectoral crisis, which is associated with the process of uneven and combined economic development, and which is almost always regarded as a particular rather than a general crisis of capital. Differences in the rate of profit between regions or countries are explained in terms of the tendency for capital to concentrate in particular areas of industrial agglomeration at the expense of other regions. The concentration of capital and uneven development occur because of external economies and economies of scale in physical and social infrastructures, and also because the rate of profit in branches of the economy dominated by large-scale capital concentrated in industrial regions is relatively high, the reason being that big capital theoretically appropriates surplus value produced by small-scale capital through the process of the equalization of profit rates. Similar arguments – for example, the theory of unequal exchange – have been applied to profit rates in the developed industrial countries compared with those in the underdeveloped regions of world economy. Combined development, in which relatively advanced technology, management systems, and forms of fixed capital employ relatively undeveloped and cheap forms of labor power, has the opposite effect: backward zones are developed by modern forms of capital at the expense of older developed industrial zones, which then become a "'reserve' of places [like] the reserve army of workers."[55] David Harvey has argued persuasively that the

---

[55] Richard Walker, "Two sources of uneven development under advanced capitalism: spatial differentiation and capital mobility," *RRPE*, 10, 3 (Fall 1978), 32–3.

cause is a combination of high congestion costs, rising rents, growing wages, and the like in the older industrial zones, and lower rents, low wages, and so on in the newer zones. In his view, neither geographic centralization nor decentralization of capital are inevitable – rather, capital continually evaluates the costs and benefits of both before making key investment/ disinvestment decisions.

Harvey also makes a theoretical connection between structural crises and sectoral crises when he argues that the latter, in part, express the spatial dimensions of the former.[56] It is widely thought, for example, that the modern structural crisis of Western capitalism in part assumes the form of the regional decline of older industrial zones (the Northeast and Midwest in the USA) and the simultaneous development of new zones (South, Southwest, and West in the USA) and new industrial centers in countries such as Brazil, Mexico, the "newly industrializing economies" of Asia, and elsewhere.[57] On the other

[56] For example, the "phases of crises are always manifest as a joint reorganization of both technologies and regional configurations to production": Harvey, *The Limits to Capital*, xiv.

Harvey's brilliant discussion of capital's spatial configurations and economic crisis is provocative as well as very useful. He shows that sectoral crises may be manifestations of general crisis arising from the tendency for the rate of profit to fall. Or they may be merely the result of a process of capital valuation/devaluation and changes in the spatial configurations of fixed capital. Harvey shows that a crisis of capital overproduction may be postponed or displaced by a "spatial fix," i.e. the export of surplus capital, surplus commodities, imports of labor, etc. This "fix," however, may not be available because of processes of capital restructuring elsewhere in the world economy (ibid., 426–7). He also shows that uneven development may *prevent* a general crisis because of "compensating oscillations within the parts" of the system as a whole (ibid., 428). His discussion of the scope and limits of the possibility of a "spatial fix" and the contradictions therein stresses the tension between "geographic inertia" arising from the capitalization of the world and the periodic need for geographic restructuring of capital, capital flexibility and mobility, etc. He concludes that a crisis in the international coordinating mechanisms of world capitalism, arising from extreme tensions between fixity and mobility of capital, leads to attempts at global economic and political reform, which may or may not succeed. The failure of such reform creates a general world crisis (ibid., 432).

[57] Froebel, Heinrichs, and Kreye, *The New International Division of Labor*; Barry Bluestone and Bennett Harrison, *Capital and Communities: The*

hand, it is also true that new and growing branches of the economy may fill the "holes" left by the decline or relocation of older industries in the traditional industrial zones, once a context of new and favorable investment climates, weakened unions, and local governments eager to attract investments has been established. In Harvey's words, "Place-specific devaluation of the capital embodied in social infrastructures, to say nothing of the destruction of traditional ways of life and all forms of localism built around social and human institutions, then becomes one of the central elements of crisis formation and resolution."[58]

All three concepts of crisis, and the different crisis theories advanced to explain them (the most important are elaborated below), share the premise that capitalism is inherently crisis-ridden. However, crisis theory departs from the medical model in that it is also based on the premise that capitalism is crisis-dependent. (That "capital accumulates through crisis" is a theme that I shall explore shortly.) In other words, crises are regarded as mechanisms whereby capitalism regulates itself: "While seeing crises as the expression of the contradiction of capitalist production . . . they represent only a temporary break in the drive to expansion, a recreation of the conditions of that expansion which have temporarily broken down, rather than a manifestation of a tendency to stagnate."[59] Some theorists argue that structural crises alone "self-construct" through processes of capital restructuring and social and political change: "What defines a situation of structural crisis is that it becomes impossible to expand or reproduce the system without

Causes and Consequences of Private Disinvestment (Washington, DC, 1980).

In the USA, sunbelt industrialization has been the result not only of cheap labor, new markets, and lower costs, but also Federal government military and highway spending bias against the North and in favor of the South. Plant closures by conglomerate capitals in the Northeast have been much higher than failure rates of independently owned plants: John C. Raines, Lenora E. Berson, and David McI. Gracie (eds), *Community and Capital in Conflict: Plant Closings and Job Loss* (Philadelphia, 1982).

[58] Harvey, *The Limits to Capital*, 403.

[59] Michael Bleaney, *Underconsumption Theories: A Historical and Critical Analysis* (New York, 1976), 110–19.

a transformation or reorganization of the basic characteristics of production, distribution and management, and their expression in terms of social organization."[60] Other writers (and there is considerable overlap between the two groups) argue that capital restructuring in the more restricted sense of the weeding out of inefficient enterprises, strengthening of larger capitals, downgrading or recomposition of labor, and so on, may also occur during the downswings and troughs of the periodic capitalist cycle.

In sum, the historical record shows clearly that Western capitalism has been convulsed by cyclical, structural, and sectoral economic transformations which have assumed varied and complex forms in different times and places. Moreover, social and economic historians have studied bouts of economic hard times as periods of capital restructuring or "self-reconstruction." Yet, while historians have often understood crises to be 'immanent" in capitalist historical development, neither the medical crisis analogy nor the historical evidence proves that capitalism is *inherently* crisis-ridden, nor still less that the system is crisis-dependent. Crisis theory has a central logical status within the problematic of orthodox and neo-orthodox theories of capital, but those who adopt this problematic must demonstrate logically that economic crises not only have happened in history but also have been historically both "inevitable" and "necessary."

Structural Origins of Economic Crisis

As we have seen, in the 1840s Engels explained economic crises in terms of capitalist "unregulated production." During the economic hard times of the late 1840s, Marx and Engels reasoned that the crisis originated in increased competition brought about by "large-scale industry" and overproduction of commodities.[61] Even earlier, in *The Poverty of Philosophy*,

---

[60] Castells, *The Economic Crisis and American Society*, 8.
[61] Marx and Engels, *Collected Works*, vol. 6, 347, 492.

Marx dismissed the standard view that there could occur a consistent "correct proportion between [commodity] supply and demand" with the rise of large-scale industry.[62] Marx returned to the theme of the effects of competition on capitalist accumulation in *Capital*: "Competition compels the replacement of the old instruments of labour by new ones before the expiration of their natural life, especially when decisive changes occur. Such premature renewals of factory equipment on a rather large social scale are mainly enforced by catastrophes or crises."[63]

As many writers have shown, Marx and Engels's early crisis theory was revolutionized with the development of the theory of surplus value in *Capital* (even though the stress on competition and the growth of large-scale industry and their implications for the accumulation process was retained). If we combine Marx's mature theory of economic exploitation and surplus-value production with his earlier concept of the "anarchy of the market," it can be concluded that economic crisis is always *latent* in capitalism. There are two closely related reasons. The first is that, because capitalist production is subject to the anarchy of the market, crisis potentials exist because of the "split between the sale and purchases" of commodities in time and space.[64] When this "split" becomes too great, a disjuncture or rupture in the process of capitalist reproduction occurs.[65] Secondly, since capitalist production is surplus-value

---

[62] Ibid., 137.

[63] Marx, *Capital*, II, 170.

[64] Marx, *Capital*, I, 113. Tugan-Baranowsky and Hilferding argued that the anarchy of the market was the source of crisis itself, not merely one kind of crisis potential. Hence they believed that state planning or organized capitalism could prevent or ameliorate crisis tendencies. A good short review of the history of the many combinations and permutations of Marxist crisis theory in the nineteenth century and early twentieth century is Russell Jacoby, "The politics of crisis theory: towards the critique of automatic Marxism, II," *Telos*, 23 (Spring 1975). A more thorough and critical review can be found in Mattick, *Economic Crisis and Crisis Theory*, chapter 3.

[65] Ben Fine, *Marx's Capital* (London, 1975), 58. A more sophisticated formulation is that the anarchy of the market also creates disparities "between the price actually obtained by and the value intrinsic to a particular commodity for sale [which] may disrupt the continued production of that

production and realization, the potential for capital overproduction exists because "the conditions of direct exploitation, and those of realizing it, are not identical. The first are
limited by the productive power of society, the latter by the
proportional relation of the various branches of production and
the consuming power of society."[66] This is a "logical" contradiction because favorable conditions of surplus-value
production, such as relatively low wage rates, imply unfavor-
able conditions of value realization, or insufficient aggregate
demand, and vice versa.[67] Capitalist exploitation is also the
focus of Marxist "class struggle" theory, which defines possibilities of crisis in terms of the "internal workings of capital
conceived as the total social relation of the two classes" (i.e.
capital and labor).[68] This means that not only economic crisis
but also class struggle is logically inherent in the capitalist
system based on surplus-value production. Capital's constant
drive to raise the rate of exploitation tends to reduce the
"consuming power of society" relative to its productive power
and simultaneously increase the level of capital–labor conflict.
In both varieties of Marxist theory, commodity production and
circulation constitute a logical contradiction because the

----

commodity and beyond that the production of commodities in general. . . .
Crises are occasions of extreme disproportion between values and prices":
Richard D. Wolff, "Marxian crisis theory: structure and implications,"
RRPE, 10, 1 (Spring 1978), 49. Wolff's article makes some interesting
observations about the relationship between capitalist expectations, different
levels of efficiency of different capitalist firms, and economic crisis.

[66] Marx, *Capital*, III, 244–5. Lebowitz regards this contradiction as the
only barrier to expansion which is specific to the capitalist mode of production, although general barriers existing in all modes of production take specific
capitalist forms, i.e. crisis ("The general and the specific in Marx's theory of
crisis," *passim*).

[67] As we shall see below, insufficient demand for commodities, according
to Marx, may be compensated for by the growth of "fictitious capital," i.e.
money capital in circulation which is not materially embodied in commodities
or productive capital but which exchanges against surplus value which *is*
embedded in commodities. Other compensations for potential deficiencies of
demand include capitalist consumption; foreign trade; export of money
capital; increased circulation expenses and state spending.

[68] Cleaver and Bell, "Marx's crisis theory as a theory of class relations,"
221.

"consuming power of society" is limited by the working class's share of total production and income which (everything else being the same) is inversely related to the "conditions of direct exploitation." Small consumption baskets and/or a low unit-value content of the average consumption basket (i.e. relatively little living labor embodied in the average consumption basket) facilitate surplus-value production but precisely for this reason obstruct the realization of values.[69] According to "class struggle" crisis theory, this establishes the conditions of speed-up, wage cuts, and unemployment, which intensify class conflict as well as the danger of overproduction of capital. By contrast, large consumption baskets and/or a high unit-value content facilitate the realization of values but limit surplus-value production. The result is the danger of one kind of underproduction of capital, which is rejected by many neo-orthodox Marxists,[70] but accepted by "class struggle" and

[69] This idea was transformed by Russian populist writers into an "underconsumption crisis" theory, which held that limited markets limited the growth of capital. There is a similarity between this view and that of the "Keynesian Marxists," who write that "as the stock of capital grows, so does productive capacity. At some point in this self-expansion of the capital stock, however, a point is reached where the effective demand for consumer goods is insufficient to warrant further investment": "Supply-side theory and capital investment," *Monthly Review* (April 1983), 3. Tugan-Baranowsky developed a critique of the Russian populist view with the argument that capital-goods production will expand *independently* of consumption if produced surplus value is invested. Lenin echoed this view when he maintained that capital-goods industries can grow independently of consumer-goods industries (Bruce McFarlane, "Lenin's revolutionary economics," *Arena*, 22 (1970). The critique of the "Keynesian Marxist" argument is, first, that surplus value is invested not only in capital goods but in labor power, hence that additions to the output side consist not only of capital goods but also of consumer goods; second, that, when profits are invested in capital goods, workers are hired to build factories, etc., hence additions to consumer demand are created. The counter-argument is that typically less capital is invested in labor power than in constant capital, especially in industries producing means of production.

Rosa Luxemburg, who was one of the first twentieth-century revolutionaries to forge a theoretical link between imperialism and crisis, argued that the development of new markets in the pre- and semi-capitalist regions of the world could postpone "underconsumption crises" at home.

[70] The reason is that, in orthodox theory, wages are assumed to depend on the rate of accumulation. If wages are "too high," accumulation slows down, unemployment increases, and wages decline. If wages are "too low,"

"profit squeeze" theorists. In sum, overproduction and this particular kind of underproduction of capital express themselves as shortages of realized profits and produced profits, respectively.

It needs to be added that the potential for overproduction (and underproduction) of capital creates disproportionalities between effective demand and commodity values in means of production and means of consumption industries. In periods of economic expansion, capital-goods production in principle grows faster than consumer-goods production. Up to a point, therefore, capital is able to "supply its own demand" (i.e. capital-goods industries supply markets for one another), thus postponing capital overproduction. Meanwhile, however, productive capacity expands more rapidly than the "consuming power of society" (especially if capital-goods production is less labor-intensive than consumer-goods production), and this increases the risk of future capital overproduction. During periods of economic contraction, capital-goods production in principle declines more rapidly than consumer-goods production. Up to a point, capital is able to "demand its own supply," thus postponing dangers of capital underproduction. However, when productive capacity contracts faster than society's "consuming power," risks of future capital underproduction are increased.

An adequate theory of economic crisis must identify not only the logical possibilities but also the logical *probabilities* of crisis within the capitalist mode of production. In neo-orthodox theory, crisis probabilities arise at two different but related levels of the accumulation process. The first pertains to overproduction of capital and the necessity for an expanding credit system;[71] the second pertains to the tendency of the rate of profit to fall. Each will be discussed in turn.

---

potentially more rapid accumulation of capital pushes the economy to higher employment and wage levels. However, wages may also be considered to be determined by the self-valorization of labor and the class struggle, as (in neo-orthodox Marxism) are hours of work.

[71] The best discussions of the role of credit in capitalism can be found in Suzanne de Brunhoff, *Marx on Money* (New York, 1976), and Harvey, *The Limits to Capital*.

As we have seen, the potential for overproduction of capital exists because "the conditions of direct exploitation, and those of realizing it, are not identical." The probability of overproduction exists because competition between individual capitals forces each to expand productive capacity beyond the limit of demand for consumer commodities. In contrast with so-called underconsumption theories of crisis, which stress absolute limits on wages and consumer demand,[72] overproduction theories state that (even though the rate of exploitation may increase) wages increase in the process of capital accumulation but not so fast as increases in real or potential productive capacity. Thus, as Marx himself showed, the development of a credit system (an "ever-lengthening chain of payments") is a required feature of capitalism. The reason is not only that the "split between the sale and purchase" of commodities in time and space requires short-term credit, or that the need to finance fixed capital requires long-term credit (or even, in the modern world, that the culture of "consumerism" requires vast amounts of consumer and mortgage credit), but that overproduction of capital requires constantly growing credit money. While the advance of credit may for a while overcome capitalism's inherent tendency toward overproduction," the credit system internalizes the contradictions of capitalism and does not abolish them."[73]

One reason is that capitalism over time develops an independent credit cycle, including the independent circulation of titles to real capital (e.g. stocks), the prices of which fluctuate independently of movements of the value of real capital.[74] The

[72] As Mattick shows, if capitalist crises were due to underconsumption, crisis resolution would depend on increasing consumption capacity in relation to production. But, typically, the resolution of economic crises does not require an increase in consumption capacity (*Economic Crisis and Crisis Theory*, 60, 65).

[73] Harvey, *The Limits to Capital*, 272.

[74] Ibid., 268. In Mandel's words, in "late capitalism" a "credit cycle temporarily distinct from the industrial cycle comes into being" ("The industrial cycle in late capitalism," 13). The theory that the credit system is governed by quasi-independent processes is also presented in de Brunhoff, *Marx on Money*, 107–18.

credit cycle thus creates not only the possibility of more severe future crises arising from the "anarchy of the market" and/or the contradiction between value production and realization but also the possibility of an independent credit crisis or credit collapse.[75] During economic booms, credit money and fictitious capital tend to grow more rapidly than real capital, thus producing a twofold realization problem – the realization of fictitious values as well as values in the commodity form.[76] Furthermore, during periods of economic expansion, interest rates rise, money capital is reallocated from industrial capital to interest-bearing capital, and capital as a whole tends to be undermined.[77] Also, credit expansion is regarded as the most important source of inflation, which "momentarily disguises the fact that expansionary forces are exhausted."[78] Finally, the growth of credit permits inefficient capitals to remain in business, thus creating more inflation because "high costs and unrealistic capital values get built into pricing structures. Similarly, credit extensions maintain high levels of employment keeping pressure on wages in all sectors of the economy."[79] In

[75] Credit creates situations in which "forced sales" or "sales to meet payments" become necessary when banks press for payments on loans during times when merchant revenues are "slow and meager" (in Marx's words). A well-developed credit system thus increases chances of a "crash" or abrupt fall in prices, including the devaluation of fixed capital.

[76] Harvey, *The Limits to Capital*, 295.

[77] Ibid., 270–1. Harvey also has a good discussion of the relation between nation-states and the credit system. He shows that credit money at one and the same time must be anchored in the power of particular nation-states and also move freely on a world scale. The nation-state is thus a *condition* of and also a *barrier* to capital (ibid., 387).

Harry Magdoff and Paul Sweezy partly explain today's high real interest rates in terms of the "enormous speculation in financial instruments" and "the circulation of credit among financial institutions" as well as "the need to attract foreign capital lest the dollar's international value collapses" (Harry Magdoff, letter to the author, June 17, 1984).

[78] Cy Gonick, "Boom and bust: state policy and the economics of restructuring," *Studies in Political Economy*, 11 (Spring 1983), 38.

[79] Ibid. Gonick argues that the "inflationary strategy" cannot work in the long run because inflation increases speculation and creates disorder in financial markets, raises interest rates, and tends to increase trade wars between capitalist nations – which, in turn, forces governments to control price levels.

sum, any and all ruptures within and between the commodity
and money circuits of capital as well as within the credit system
itself manifest themselves in realization and/or liquidity crises
depending on the exact conjuncture of the industrial and credit
cycles.[80]

In neo-orthodox Marxist thought, the second (and most
debated) perspective on economic crisis is the theory of the
falling rate of profit. This theory is generally discussed in terms
which include problems of credit, monopoly, international
trade, and so on, but it is convenient for expository purposes to
evaluate this perspective at least in part independently. In
Capital, Marx stressed that the falling profit rate was merely a
"tendency" which requires "long periods" for its "effects" to

---

[80] Another and closely related internal contradiction of capital pertains to
the credit system and the development of fixed capital and the built environment, including the physical and social infrastructure. Harvey's discussion of
this internal barrier is highly recommended. Only some highlights will be
noted here.

Fixed capital reduces capitalism's flexibility. In Harvey's words, "The
barrier fixed capital creates to future accumulation can be overcome only by
way of the credit system in particular" (ibid., 269). Further, "To the degree
that interest-bearing capital becomes committed to specific use values, it loses
its co-ordinating powers because it loses its flexibility" (ibid., 266). With
regard to transportation capital, "the value embodied in the produced space of
the transport system becomes the barrier to overcome. The preservation of
particular use values within the transport network means constraints to the
further expansion of value in general. Strong devaluation and restructuring
within the transport system . . . then becomes inevitable. This is the central
contradiction which modifies and circumscribes the mobility of capital in the
commodity form" (ibid., 380). As for the spatial distribution of technology
and crisis, "A break with past technological mixes and spatial configurations
often entails massive devaluation. But failure to 'rationalize' technological
mixes and spatial configurations underlies crises of accumulation in the first
place" (ibid., 394). Further, the social infrastructure (education, etc.) has to be
periodically restructured in space and form, a process accompanied by crises.
"Place-specified devaluation of the capital embodied in social infrastructures,
to say nothing of the destruction of traditional ways of life and all forms of
localism built around social and human institutions, then becomes one of the
central elements of crisis formation and resolution" (ibid., 403). Finally,
Harvey stresses that "crises . . . unfold with differential effects" geographically because "excess profits at one place will be gained at the expense of
devaluation losses elsewhere" (ibid., 394).

become "strikingly pronounced."[81] Yet, since the systematic development of this theory by Henryk Grossman in 1929, many if not most neo-orthodox Marxists argue that the falling profit rate is the "ultimate" barrier to capitalist accumulation.[82]

In the typical approach to the subject, cyclical and secular movements in the profit rate are analyzed separately. Cyclical ups and downs in profits and the business cycle are explained in terms of the uneven development of capital- and consumer-goods production. By contrast, and more important in the corpus of Marxist theory, long-run declines in the rate of profit are deduced from the relationship between certain key socio-economic categories developed in *Capital*. These categories are: first, the organic composition of capital (C/V, or the ratio of "dead" to living, socially necessary labor); and, second, the rate of exploitation (S/V, or the ratio of surplus labor to socially necessary labor). Constant capital (C) symbolizes the mass of means of production (K) and the unit value of the means of production (vK). Variable capital (V) stands for total employment (L) and the unit value of labor power, i.e. the average consumption basket (vL). K/L is defined as the technical composition of capital; vK/vL alone is the value composition of capital.[83]

[81] Marx, *Capital*, III, 237–9.

[82] In a comprehensive review of Marxist crisis theory, Al Szymanski has argued that the majority of twentieth-century theorists accepted an over-production theory of crisis, not the theory of the falling profit rate ("The overproduction theory of economic crisis," MS, March 1983). The citations below show, however, that there are many Marxist political economists today who accept some version of the theory of the falling profit rate.

[83] Put another way, C/V is the ratio of constant to variable capital and S/V is the ratio of surplus value to variable capital. "Constant capital" consists of plant and equipment, raw materials, fuels, water, etc. used in the production and reproduction of plant and equipment. "Variable capital" consists of human labor power. The money form of "constant capital" is depreciation and amortization funds together with monies used to replace raw materials, fuels, and the like used up in production. The money form of "variable capital" consists of wages and fringes. "Surplus value" is the value of commodities over and above the value required to reproduce constant capital and the employed workforce in its present or given material state. "Surplus value" may be accumulated in the form of additional constant and/or variable

The rate of profit, hence the potential rate of accumulation (or the rate at which surplus value can be converted into more capital), is defined as $S/C+V$, or $S/C/V+1$. According to this formula, the rate of profit varies directly with the rate of exploitation and inversely with the organic composition of capital. The composition of capital and the rate of exploitation are thus two key variables in Marx's theory of the declining profit rate. A third variable is the turnover time of capital, or the sum of the time of production and time of circulation, i.e. the average production period and average time lapse between production and sale of commodities. Turnover time depends on many factors: technological and organizational changes in production, transport, and communications; sales expenses and credit; the level of consumer demand, and so on. In short, turnover time is the speed at which money capital can be successfully "metamorphized" into productive capital and commodity capital and, finally, more money capital. The final key variable in the determination of the rate of profit is the cost of material elements entering into constant and variable capital, e.g. raw materials and energy costs.[84]

In neo-orthodox theory, the main variable in the theory of the falling profit rate is the organic composition of capital. This is so because the main "rule" in capitalist production (assuming wage and other costs remain unchanged) is the maximization of increases in production per unit of labor time, i.e., technical change, speed-up, etc. hence the constant "expulsion" of living labor from the production process. In "class struggle" crisis theory, the rate of exploitation is given more or less equal weight. However, in the most "rigorous" versions of neo-

---

capital; used for speculative purposes; taxed by the state; etc. The "unit value of means of production (vK)" is the amount of living labor required to reproduce constant capital defined in physical terms. The "unit value of labor power (vL)" is the amount of living labor required to reproduce the present or given bundle of consumer goods which enter into the consumption of the employed working class.

[84] The analysis of the costs of the elements of capital requires a discussion of rent theory, which is indispensable to any full account of the theory of "nature" as an "external barrier" (Harvey, *The Limits to Capital*, chapter 11, sections I–VI).

orthodox Marxism, the class struggle and the rate of exploitation are regarded as secondary factors. In fact, in Marx's own view, increases in the composition of capital (C/V) are associated with *increases* in relative surplus value and the rate of exploitation (S/V). At a certain point in the accumulation of capital, however, increases in the former are thought to be greater than increases in the latter (see below). In Marx's words, "the rate of profit does not fall because labor becomes less productive, but because labor becomes more productive."[85] In short, the rate of profit falls despite the fact that the rate of exploitation (as well as the mass of surplus value and profits) increases or remains constant.

Ernest Mandel has applied this general line of reasoning to economic crisis tendencies in the 1960s and early 1970s in his influential book, *Late Capitalism*.[86] Mandel stressed the development after World War II of a "third industrial revolution," or the spread of modern technology into new spheres of the economy, and also the declining costs of the elements of constant and variable capital (e.g. oil) during the heyday of the "American century." According to Mandel, until the 1960s, the average value composition of capital declined because economic sectors which were not previously highly capitalized absorbed the lion's share of new money capital advanced. However, beginning in the 1960s, the rapid capitalization of agriculture, commerce, and services resulted in a sharp rise in the organic composition of capital. Capital was thus compelled to raise the rate of exploitation to compensate for the increase in the composition of capital and to maintain the rate of profit, which in turn ignited the flames of the workers' struggle in the late 1960s and early 1970s.

Mandel concluded that Western capitalism in this way reached a temporary impasse. On the one hand, if the capital stock was deepened, i.e. expansion of capital based on an

[85] Marx, *Capital*, III, 240. This is neo-orthodoxy's basic critique of "profits squeeze" theories of crisis, which maintain that the rate of profit falls because the rate of exploitation declines (Peter Howell, "Once again on productive and unproductive labour," *Revolutionary Communist*, 3–4 (1975), 57).

[86] Ernest Mandel, *Late Capitalism*.

increase in K/L, the reserve army of labor would be reconstituted, which would shift the balance of power against the working class, but which would also increase the composition of capital to even higher levels. At the limit, a strategy of full automation would mean that the mass of surplus value (not only the rate of profit) would be "tendentially condemned to diminish." Put another way, the composition of capital would be so high that no conceivable rate of exploitation would suffice to prevent the profit rate from falling.[87] Mandel also argued that an "automation strategy" would intensify the class struggle over the rate of exploitation. On the other hand, if the capital stock was widened, i.e. expansion of capital based on the given ratio of K/L, the value composition of capital would be held in check, but the rate of exploitation would remain low or even decline because the demand for labor would rise sharply and the reserve army of labor would dry up more or less completely. Mandel believed that capital's only practical strategy was an investment strike – that is, a smaller level of capital formation, relative economic stagnation, and a decade or two of short cyclical upswings and long recessions. This crude review of the thesis of the master of neo-orthodox Marxism makes clear that *Late Capitalism* remained solidly in the traditionalist camp. Mandel retained the orthodox focus on changes in the composition of capital and explained attempts to raise the rate of exploitation as a possible offset to increases in the former, rather than vice versa.[88]

[87] Ibid., 204.

[88] The thesis that the organic composition of capital rose in the 1960s was contested by Bob Rowthorn, who argued that there is little or no evidence that the value composition of capital had risen either in the short or long run: "Review of *Late Capitalism*," *New Left Review*, 98 (July–August 1976). He agreed with Mandel that the technical composition of capital increased after World War II, but presented evidence to the effect that the value composition did not. Rowthorn's argument also applied to the work of Gamble and Walton, who agreed with Mandel that the low value composition of capital after World War II created favorable conditions for a rising profit rate, but that the development of electronics, computers, and other new industries which had large labor-saving effects on the economy as a whole finally raised the value composition and lowered the profit rate: Andrew Gamble and Paul Walton, *Capitalism in Crisis: Inflation and the State* (London, 1976).

The neo-orthodox theory of the falling profit rate is regarded by most if not all neo-orthodox Marxists as indispensable to any "scientific" understanding of the modern crisis of capitalism. This theory has important political overtones because it implies that open class struggle is a reaction to capital's attempts to raise the rate of exploitation (see chapter 3). For these reasons, the neo-orthodox view requires some elaboration, especially with regard to its central premise, which is that, while the source of capitalist profit is surplus value, the connection between the rate of exploitation and rate of profit is an indirect and fetishized one. The argument is that the composition of capital mediates the relation between exploitation and profit, hence the relationship between the profit rate and capital accumulation. Increases in the composition of capital result from the integration of science and technology into industry, and the replacement of living labor by "dead" labor. Only living labor, however, produces surplus value. Marxists describe this contradiction thus: "It is a contradictory feature of capital that individual profit is pursued by reducing values through relative expulsion of living labor, which is the source of surplus value, from production."[89]

According to neo-orthodox theory, capitalism destroys its own capacity to increase surplus-value production (hence negates its capacity for self-expansion) for two general reasons. The first is that there exists an absolute limit on exploitation, given the limit on the length of the working day, on the number of workers, and on reductions in the size of the average consumption basket (although not the unit-value content of the consumption basket, which theoretically may approach zero). These physical and social facts place limits on both the rate and mass of surplus value. The second reason is that the costs of reproducing constant capital on an increasingly expanding scale progressively increase.

At a high stage of accumulation, value demanded for additional constant capital [must be] so great that it finally absorbs all of the

---

[89] Fine, *Marx's Capital*, 55.

surplus-value. A point must come when the parts of surplus-value to be used for additional workers and for capitalist consumption must decrease absolutely. This would be the turning point at which the previously latent tendency to collapse begins to be active.[90]

In other words, constant capital finally assumes such a large proportion of total capital that a relatively small amount of society's labor time produces surplus value, because more labor time is required to reproduce constant capital on an expanded scale. Accordingly, "the falling rate of profit is an absolute, ultimate barrier which cannot be surpassed by increases in productivity (relative surplus value) or extensions of the workday (absolute surplus value). The declining rate of . . . profit is a Limit to the production of surplus value, a Limit immanent in production."[91]

The reader will note that until now little has been said about the realization of profits, only their production. The importance of the problem of market sales, or realizing profits, is underscored in Marx's famous passage, "the more productiveness develops, the more it finds itself at variance with the narrow basis on which the condition of consumption rests."[92] This problem of "realization of values" is reinforced by the accelerated obsolescence of fixed capital arising from technological change, which forces individual capitals to replace means of production before they have transferred all of their embodied value to commodities.[93] In Castells's words, "Capital needs more and more time to realize the value invested in fixed capital but allows itself less and less time to do so."[94]

[90] Paul Mattick, "The permanent crisis: Henry K. Grossman's interpretation of Marx's theory of capitalist accumulation," *International Council Correspondence*, 2 (November 1934), 7.

[91] Michael Lebowitz, "Marx's falling rate of profit: a dialectical view," *Socialist Review*, 38 (8, 2) (March–April 1978), 86. In the Grossman–Mattick version, not only the rate of profit but also the mass of profits must sooner or later fall.

[92] Marx, *Capital*, III, 245.

[93] Monopolies may try to preserve the value of their fixed capital, and hence function as a barrier to technological innovation.

[94] Castells, *The Economic Crisis and American Society*, 56.

Michael Lebowitz sums up the problem of the relationship between value production and realization in this way:

The drive of capital to expand the production of surplus value by reducing necessary labor relative to surplus labor and the number of workers relative to means of production creates barriers to the realization of capital [as well as the production of capital]. A gap opens up, a gap between the productive power of society and the consuming power. Rising circulation time reflects this growth gap; it reflects the difficulty of selling. . . . It is the increase in circulation time which leads to the crisis: "The crisis occurs not only because the commodity is unsaleable, but because it is not saleable within a *particular period of time.*"[95]

This problem may be temporarily resolved if more capital is allocated to the sphere of circulation (e.g. advertising and other marketing expenses), thus reducing circulation time and postponing or preventing a "realization crisis." In most neo-orthodox thought, capital allocated to "unproductive government expenditures" has a similar effect. In this event, more capital is utilized unproductively, which at some stage in the accumulation process increases the risk of underproduction of capital. Capitalism is thus inevitably poised on the knife-edge of crises of traditionally defined overproduction and underproduction of capital. Only the expansion of credit money or "fictitious capital" permits the system to solve its realization crisis tendency without at the same time starving productive capital as a result of the unproductive utilization of capital in the sphere of circulation, capitalist consumption, and/or state expenditures.[96] This "solution," however, means that new

---

[95] Lebowitz, "Marx's falling rate of profit," 90, quoting Marx, *Theories of Surplus Value*, III (London, 1952).

[96] "Fictitious capital," as we have seen, is money which circulates as capital without having any material basis in commodity or productive capital.

An interesting variation of this theory is Joseph Gillman's in *The Falling Rate of Profit* (London, 1957), and *Prosperity in Crisis* (New York, 1965). Gillman begins with the premise that modern monopolies restrict production and new investment, meanwhile maintaining high and rising prices – which creates a big gap between production and investment potential and effective

credit money is constantly being created which must be "real-ized" in expanded material production: hence capital's obsession with perpetually increased growth and accumulation and, inferentially, the capitalist state's obsession with opening land, natural resources, labor power, and markets on a global scale for capitalist exploitation.

Marx and neo-orthodox Marxists argue that the contradiction between value production and realization, the rise in the composition of capital, and limits on increases in the rate of exploitation express themselves in the tendential law of the falling rate of profit. This "law" is regarded as a systemic phenomenon which individual capitalists, workers, and others merely personify. Individual capitalists are blind to the ways that their uncoordinated actions and uncontrolled need to expand are connected with either overproduction or under-production of capital. Individual capitals must "expand or die," even when they are aware of the "unintentional effects" of their actions. Under normal conditions, they expect constant or rising profit rates, hence steady or increased rates of economic expansion, and they expand production of means of production and means of consumption accordingly. Fresh capi-

---

demand for commodities. On the one hand, this strategy keeps a lid on the organic composition of capital; on the other hand, it requires increasing amounts of "unproductive and unreproductive consumption" financed by debt or "spurious capital." In Jacob Morris's words, "According to the Gillman theory, monopoly capitalism behaves just as if it felt in its bones the profound truth of Marx's law of the falling tendency of the rate of profit. It behaves as if it knew that the uninhibited actualization of its vast potential for real physical capital would land it in the iron grip of that law. It seeks to escape this fate by inhibiting the expansion of physical or constant capital (C), by consequently inhibiting increases in the organic composition of capital (C/V), by substituting unproductive expenditures (U) for C, and by thus replacing C/V by U/V. Instead of an increasing organic composition of capital, monopoly capitalism gives us an increasing ratio of unproductive expenditure to productive wages. Instead of the classic Marxist form of the falling rate of profit tendency related to an increasing organic composition of capital, monopoly capitalism gives us a new, pathological form of the law of the falling profit tendency which is related to an increasing ratio of unproductive to productive expenditure": Jacob Morris, "Underconsumption and the general crisis: Gillman's theory," *Science and Society*, 47, 3 (Fall, 1983), 327.

tal is produced with the expectation that other capitals will enlarge or modernize their facilities, purchase new equipment and raw materials, and expand employment. When the rise in the composition of capital causes the profit rate to decline, the flow of money capital sooner or later becomes too small to permit individual capitals to reproduce existing capital and/or purchase additional constant and circulating capital. (Exactly when this "turning point" occurs theoretically depends on the values which theorists assign to the key variables in the accumulation model.) The final result is an unplanned expansion of inventories of commodities and/or excess productive capacity;[97] a wave of general pessimism; a weakening or collapse of the credit structure; and a general crisis and economic contraction. "The anarchy of capitalist production makes crisis possible but the falling rate of profit makes it inevitable. This is because a crisis is the social outcome of the interaction of pessimistic capitalists' individual decisions, whereas a falling rate of profit is the social outcome that makes these decisions certain."[98]

Many Marxist and non-Marxist economists have been skeptical about the tendential law of the falling rate of profit and have attempted to refute it on the grounds that its premises are unrealistic and/or that it is logically inconsistent or confusing.[99]

[97] "The crises of 'realization' which characterize capitalism are not crises of . . . sale of already produced goods but of . . . self-expansion of capital": Patrick Clawson, "A comment on Van Parijs' obituary," *RRPE*, 15, 2 (Summer 1983), 108.

[98] Fine, *Marx's Capital*, 58.

[99] For example, Philippe Van Parijs, "The falling-rate-of-profit theory of crisis: a rational reconstruction by way of an obituary," *RRPE*, 12, 1 (Spring 1980). The distinction between effective demand for replacement of means of production and consumption, on the one hand, and demand for additional means of production and consumption, on the other, seems to be ignored in this detailed attack on the theory of the falling profit rate (ibid., £9). A detailed critique of Van Parijs's work is Clawson, "A comment on Van Parijs' obituary." Another new critique is Al Szymanski, "A requiem for the law: an analysis of the rising organic composition of capital/tendency of the profit rate to fall," MS (January 1983). Szymanski takes great pains to show that, until Henryk Grossman's work in the late 1920s, mainstream Marxism practically

The most common argument against the falling rate of profit theory (one which Marx himself was sensitive to) is that new investment in fixed capital actually increases the technical composition of capital (or K/L, where K stands for the mass of means of production and L symbolizes total employment), not the value composition of capital (or vK/vL, where vK is the unit value of means of production and vL is the unit value of labor power or the average consumption basket). The claim is that increases in the technical composition of capital, or a rise in the amount of machinery per worker (i.e. a general rise in the physical productivity per worker), may or may not increase the value composition. It is granted that (everything else being the same), if the unit value of labor power falls or remains unchanged, a rise in the technical composition of capital necessarily increases the organic composition of capital. But everything else may not remain the same. New machinery which increases the technical composition of capital (K/L) may (it is argued) reduce the value of means of production (vK) to the same degree or more than the value of means of consumption (vL). In this event, the organic composition of capital (C/V) will not rise, but remain constant or decline.

Logically, this criticism appears to be sound. In fact, it is weak. The reason pertains to the different sources of social demand for commodities produced in capital-goods compared with consumer-goods industries. Social demand for consumer goods is governed by working-class demand for means of subsistence and the mass market. Thus it is not only desirable but possible for capitals producing consumer commodities to employ techniques of mass production. These techniques tend continuously to lower the value content of consumer goods (vL). By contrast, the social demand for capital goods is

---

ignored the sections in chapters 13–15 in *Capital*, III, which work out the theory of the falling profit rate.

In the interests of brevity and clarity, I ignore arguments against Marx's profit theory which confuse profits strictly defined and "profit" arising when individual capitals get a jump on their competitors via cost-cutting innovations – "profit" which is actually a kind of "technological rent" – and concentrate on "classical" Marxist arguments and counter-arguments.

governed by the demand formed by capitals in both consumer- and capital-goods industries for high levels of profit. Greater profits typically require higher and higher levels of production per unit of labor time, which, in turn, require innovative forms of both fixed and circulating constant capital, i.e. new technologies, new machinery, and so on, which, precisely because they are new, typically have a relatively high average value content (vK). Put another way, consumer goods are ordinarily produced for mass consumption on the world market; capital goods are more often produced on special order and tailored to meet the specific needs of individual capitals and/or industries, especially industries producing capital goods.[100] The argument that technical change reduces the value of means of production as much as or more than that of means of consumption fails to grasp the fundamentally different social origin of the demand for commodities produced in the two basic branches of the economy. In general terms, capital's inherent drive to lower the value content of the average consumption basket is precisely the mechanism which permits the size of the average worker's consumption basket *and* the rate of exploitation to rise simultaneously – which Marx regarded as inherent in the general process of capitalist accumulation.

A related criticism of the falling rate of profit theory also pertains to the nature of technical change. The argument is that technical change embodied in new means of production not only may reduce the value of means of production (vK) but also may not even increase the technical composition of capital (K/L).[101] In other words, technical change may be "capital-

---

[100] In Mandel's words, new equipment "must be constructed with pre-existent machinery and pre-given techniques, *and its own value* is thus determined by present labour productivity . . . and since this equipment cannot be mass-produced in the initial stages" the assumption that productivity growth in means of production industries is more rapid than in the economy as a whole is not tenable (*Late Capitalism*, 202–3). Mandel's case can be strengthened by adding that technical change designed to raise productivity in consumer-goods industries may not raise productivity in capital-goods industries at all. A problem with Mandel's formulation may be that it conflates the issue of changes in its technical composition (see below).

[101] Gillman, *The Falling Rate of Profit*, 57.

saving" in the sense that the mass of machinery per worker may decline owing to improvements in existing fixed capital, lighter materials, and so on. It is true that many examples of "capital-saving" innovations may be found in the economic history of Western capitalism. It is also true that such innovations have the ultimate function of lowering the value of labor power (vL), i.e. increasing surplus value relatively. It is further true that modern information technology is displacing labor at a growing rate in the service and information sectors of the economy. The counter-argument is that, if the organic composition of capital in either capital- and/or consumer-goods industries is relatively high, capitalists have more incentive to economize on constant capital by discovering techniques which lower the technical composition capital. This argument has considerable force (e.g. the development of energy-saving devices by business in the USA in the 1970s). But it is important to stress that a high composition of capital historically has been associated with a developed and organized working class with some structural power over wages, hours, and working conditions. Moreover, at some stage in its development, capital must face a finite supply of labor power which, unlike fixed and circulating constant capital, cannot be produced and reproduced capitalis-tically.[102] For these reasons, capital has that much more incentive to expel living labor from production with the unin-tentional result of raising the organic composition of capital even more.

Still another criticism of the falling profit rate theory is that an increase in the technical composition of capital may reduce the costs of raw materials, fuels, and other natural elements of constant capital and in this way inhibit or reverse the tendency of the rate of profit to fall.[103] For example, new mining

[102] Thus, in Lebowitz's account, a general barrier to expansion in any mode of production assumes a specific capitalist form, namely, falling profits and crisis tendencies.

[103] Phillip Armstrong writes that Marx "gives no reason why the cheapening of the elements of constant capital could not permanently prevent the rate of profit from falling": "Accumulation of capital, the rate of profit, and crisis," *BCSE*, 4, 2 (11) (June 1975), 4. Donald Harris also sounds the warning that "a problem arises when we take into account the fact that an

machinery may cheapen raw materials, or energy-saving equipment may be installed in new or modernized production facilities. However, cheap raw materials and energy directly or indirectly sooner or later find their way into consumer-goods industries and cheapen the average consumption basket. Whether cheaper raw materials or fuels reduce the value of constant capital more or less than the value of variable capital (or wage goods) depends in part on the technical characteristics of the raw materials and fuels themselves. For example, certain kinds of hardening metals may be used mainly or wholly in capital-goods industries. Yet it remains true that raw materials used exclusively in capital-goods production will indirectly lower the value of the average consumption basket. To argue otherwise is to argue away social reproduction as a whole, or the material and economic relationship between capital and consumer-goods production.

A final point in this connection pertains to the emphasis that Marx placed on the "growing requirements of raw materials per worker, the second aspect of the technical composition of capital."[104] He also believed that capital would face barriers to increases in productivity in raw materials industries and concluded that there was a tendency for the value of means of production to increase.[105] More raw materials per worker, more expensive raw materials, he argued, would drive up the organic composition of capital. The history of twentieth-century capitalism, however, has shown that raw materials and energy (particularly when energy costs are high) have been not only produced but also used more efficiently in industry and commerce. Synthetics, less durable consumer commodities, etc., have inhibited the trend toward "growing requirements of

---

increasing mass of means of production is usually accompanied by a decreasing value of commodities including the elements of constant capital. In that case, the increasing mass may or may not be offset by the decreasing value. This leaves the direction of change ambiguous" (letter to the writer, March 1, 1980).

[104] Lebowitz, "The general and the specific in Marx's theory of crisis," 9.

[105] Ibid., 9–13. Lebowitz argues that these are general barriers in all modes of production, but under capitalism assume the specific form of economic crisis or crisis tendencies.

raw materials per worker." Energy-efficient production techniques have reduced the costs of energy per unit of production. It seems safe to conclude that Marx's views on this subject, however valid in his own time, underrated capital's genius for the efficient exploitation and utilization of raw materials, fuels, and other elements of constant as well as variable capital. Nevertheless, capital's well-known resistance to internalizing the external or environmental costs of accumulation (i.e. to either preserving or cleaning up the natural environment) means that sooner or later the costs of most if not all of the elements of constant and variable capital must rise (e.g. hard woods, clean water, etc.). If this is the case, under the restrictive assumptions of the neo-orthodox theory of accumulation and crisis, the rate of profit is likely to fall because of the rise in the value composition (hence organic composition) of capital, hence that economic crisis is not merely logically possible but also historically probable in the course of capitalist accumulation. During boom periods, a critical point is reached at which the composition of capital increases sharply while the rate of exploitation remains constant or declines as a result of labor shortages and/or working-class victories on the wages and hours front. The result is an "absolute overproduction of capital" followed by a "steep and sudden fall in the general rate of profit." In the subsequent contractions, possibilities of profitably exploiting labor decline, and this leads to cumulative reductions in production, employment, wage income, and spending. The greater the increase in the organic composition of capital during periods of economic expansion, and the higher the level of employment and the lower the rate of exploitation, the more sudden and widespread are layoffs, bankruptcies, and other features of economic crisis.[106]

To sum up this line of argument, neo-orthodox Marxist theory holds that increases in the technical composition of capital (K/L) lower the value content of the consumption basket. This means that increases in the technical composition

---

[106] For a sharp discussion of these and related issues, see Armstrong, "Accumulation of capital, the rate of profit, and crisis."

of capital indirectly raise the rate of exploitation, assuming that wages and hours of work remain unchanged. The increase in the rate of exploitation moderates the adverse effects of the rise in the organic composition of capital on the rate of profit. In terms of the theory of capitalist *production*, therefore, the rate of profit *must* fall only when the size of the average consumption basket increases more rapidly than the decline in its value content, or when its value content as well as absolute size increases. This latter possibility, which has been theorized in a "revisionist" work by the present writer, will be discussed briefly below.[107]

It is important to stress that this line of analysis remains limited because it presupposes that there is no structural gap between value production and value realization. However, as we have seen, the essence of capitalism is precisely the contradiction between the production and realization of value, i.e. the exploitation of labor.[108] This means that, sooner or later in the course of the accumulation process, the realized profit rate must decline.[109] The reason is twofold: on the one hand, if the value content and/or size of the consumption basket declines, the actual rate of profit will fall because of overproduction of capital. This is called a "crisis of realization." On the other hand, if capital is used unproductively to expand markets and shorten circulation time, more capital becomes in effect constant capital, i.e. capital which does not produce surplus value. In this event, capital will suffer a "liquidity crisis" and the actual rate of profit will fall because of underproduction of capital. As Lebowitz writes, "the decline in the rate of profit is the way in

---

[107] James O'Connor, *Accumulation Crisis* (Oxford, 1984), *passim*.

[108] Lebowitz, "Marx's falling rate of profit."

[109] Harvey underscores the importance of the turnover time of capital as well as the form of capitalist organization for the determination of the value composition of capital (which have been neglected in the discussion in this chapter for the sake of simplicity) with his concept of "realization": "All crises are crises of realization" in the sense of not only the failure to realize values in the market, but also the failure to realize money capital through production and production capital in the commodity form (*The Limits to Capital*, 129–32).

which the contradiction between production and circulation of capital expresses itself. It is no more possible to eliminate from Marx's argument the tendency for the rate of profit to fall than it is to eliminate the sphere of circulation."[110]

The neo-orthodox theory of economic crises based on either capital overproduction or the tendential decline in the rate of profit may have been plausible in the context of nineteenth-century capitalism and the "idea of progress" but appears to be less relevant today. The basic problem with neo-orthodox crisis theory is that it lacks any theory of historical class composition and recomposition, class struggle, and combined and uneven development, including the effects of class struggle on the accumulation process.[111] The "inevitability" of the falling profit rate, the idea that capital is subject to certain "laws of motion," and the underlying assumption of the theory, namely, that individuals are mere personifications of the categories of capital, are inconsistent with the massive irrationalities of twentieth-century capitalism and imperialism, including and especially the complex historical contingencies created by worldwide national and class struggles. In the late twentieth century, the masses of the world are influencing the course of history in more powerful ways than ever before, albeit in reified and distorted forms.

Neo-orthodox theory also typically downplays the analyses of writers such as Eduard Bernstein who, in the late 1890s, pointed to new structural changes in capitalism – the effects of unions on wages and prices, monopolies, and capitalist planning – which are counterweights to the crisis tendencies originally identified by Marx. The contributions of the "Keynesian Marxists" such as Michael Kalecki and Paul Sweezy also have been subject to sharp attacks by neo-orthodoxy. Another

---

[110] Lebowitz, "Marx's falling rate of profit," 90. Harvey deals with this issue with the concept of an "equilibrium share of wages in total values" (*The Limits to Capital*, 174). Departures from equilibrium result in a crisis of circulation "that can strike either in the sphere of exchange or in the sphere of production, depending upon whether wages [move] above or below their equilibrium value" (ibid.).

[111] O'Connor, *Accumulation Crisis*, chapters 2–3.

problem is that Marxist orthodoxy typically neglects the material and ideological conditions of social reproduction (although there has been more or less consistent recognition of the indirectly productive role of scientists and others whose knowledge and social labor have become the most powerful productive forces). The traditional argument ignores the possibility that conditions of social reproduction may change in ways which increase the value content and size of the consumption basket (not to speak of the social wage and its "value content"), hence that the profit rate will fall not because the composition of capital is too high, but because the rate of exploitation is too low. Traditional objectivist Marxism often ignores the implications of its own theoretical premise that the accumulation of capital is the "accumulation of proletariat," and therefore that the capacity of an expanding working class to resist increases in exploitation may grow over time. The emphasis, at least, of traditional theory is that human labor power is successfully treated as if it were merely an object of exchange and labor, and that workers thus have little or no power to reverse, much less redefine, the process of self-expanding capital except in the event of a socialist revolution. This premise denies the powerful material effects of capitalist ideologies of social and labor control and the use that "special interests" and individuals make of them. Moreover, neo-orthodox theory too often assumes that capitalist competition and class struggle compel capital to develop and deploy technology solely to lower the value content of the means of consumption. The possibility that technological change may be oriented to new consumer products with relatively high-value contents and that a vast private and public credit system may function to redistribute produced values to the working class and salariat is rarely if ever considered.[112]

The great virtue of the opposing "class struggle" theory of economic crisis is that it recognizes that human labor power is not only an object but also a subject of exchange and labor. "The quantity of value of the necessary part of the working day

[112] Ibid., *passim.*

is not only more and more rigid, but it also tends to diminish – subjectively, actively – the surplus value that can be extorted ... the devaluation of labor power ... is ... not only not indefinite, but is, on the contrary, limited and reversible."[113] In sum, it is a plausible conclusion that in the context of modern conditions of social reproduction, monopolies, product competition, consumer and public credit, and so on, and especially in the context of modern state economic and social regulation, the focus of crisis theory needs to be shifted from changes in the composition of capital and their effect on the rate of profit to the complex issues of social and national struggles and their effect on the rate of exploitation and on capital's political and social capacity to utilize labor power as variable capital, hence on the rate of profit.

Structural Functions of Economic Crisis

Theories of the historical origins of particular social processes and structures cannot normally serve as explanations of the historical functions of these same processes and structures. This standard warning in social-theoretical work also applies to theories of the structural origins and functions of capitalist economic crisis. The argument that the contradiction between value production and realization and/or the falling profit rate constitute the source of economic crises cannot be used to prove that capital accumulates *through* crises – that is, that capitalism is not only crisis-ridden but also crisis-dependent. It is to this subject we now turn.

The process of crisis-resolution is social and qualitative as well as economic and quantitative in nature. The course of any crisis, including its "final" outcome, depends not only on adjustments in the quantitative relationships between the main variables in the accumulation model (e.g. devaluation of capital, reductions in wages, etc.) but also on "adjustments" in the disturbed relationships between individual capitals and the

[113] Negri, *Marx Beyond Marx*, 101.

capital–labor relationships (e.g. capital's need to restore a favorable relationship between necessary and surplus labor). Marx himself stressed that accumulation consists not only of the expansion of capitalist wealth, but also of the development of a capitalistic labor process, concentration and centralization of capital, industrial relocation, uneven development, and so on. He argued that these kinds of qualitative changes do not and cannot occur smoothly but require periodic ruptures in the circuit of capital. (Modern-day Marxists argue that qualitative changes in social institutions, forms of state interventionism, etc., require long-term structural crises.) "A crisis always forms the starting point of large new investments," Marx wrote.[114] Crises force the introduction of new production methods, takeovers and mergers between capital units, reorganization of labor markets, industrial relocation, and so on. Crises are regarded as external, objective forces which compel individual capitals and industries to restructure themselves to prepare for a new wave of capital accumulation. In this sense, qualitative changes in the forms of capital and social reproduction as a whole during crises and depressions theoretically transform themselves into quantitative changes during recoveries and booms (which sooner or later self-destruct, forcing more qualitative changes). "Without contradiction, no movement; without the falling rate of profit, no innovation, no rising productivity of labor."[115] A crucial point of departure between bourgeois economics and Marxism, therefore, is that within the latter tradition there is general agreement that capitalism is not only crisis-ridden but also crisis-dependent.[116] Crises are the cauldrons in which capital qualitatively restructures itself for

---

[114] Marx, *Capital*, II, 186.

[115] Lebowitz, "Marx's falling rate of profit," 93.

[116] The best-known bourgeois economist in the nineteenth century who did argue that the cause of depression was prosperity, and vice versa, was Clement Juglar, whose book on "commercial crises" was published in 1862.

The major bourgeois economists in the twentieth century who dealt with the problem of the capitalist cycle and crises in a serious way were Joseph Schumpeter and Wesley Mitchell, whose work Schumpeter greatly admired. They were also two of the very few economists who emphasized qualitative changes in the process of growth. Schumpeter stressed "creative destruction"

economic, social, and political renewal and further accumulation.

Neo-orthodox Marxists disagree with regard to the exact connection between structural sources and functions of crisis (i.e. the mechanisms which restore conditions of profitable accumulation) and also question whether crises and capital restructuring in fact overcome the tendency of the rate of profit to fall. The most general area of disagreement concerns the relationship between crisis theory and the so-called offsetting or counteracting tendencies to the falling rate of profit. Besides the devaluation of constant capital arising from technological changes in production methods, these tendencies include the manipulation of the terms of trade between industrial and raw-material-supplying countries and the cheapening of raw materials; industrial relocation to "cheap-labor havens"; wage cuts below the value of labor power; and increased intensity of work.[117] Some theorists argue that these and other offsetting tendencies *postpone* economic crises; others claim that they help to *resolve* crises. What is clear is that any or all offsetting tendencies may be crisis-resolving (as well as crisis-postponing)

---

as the engine of growth (modern ecological economists call this "destructive creation"). Mitchell stressed the role of depressions in stimulating the rationalization of production processes: *Business Cycles: The Problem and its Setting* (New York, 1927); *Business Cycles and Their Causes* (Berkeley, Cal., 1963).

[117] David Harvey adds to this list increases in the industrial reserve army which encourage reproduction of low-wage capitals with a low organic composition of capital (*The Limits to Capital*, 178). He also lists the factors which Marx discusses in the *Grundrisse* which may stabilize the rate of profit and hence prevent crises (ibid., citing *Grundrisse*, 750–1). These include the devaluation of existing capital (or "planned obsolescence"); investment in fixed capital, such as public works, which is not used in direct production; unproductive expenditures; new branches of production, which typically have in the beginning a low organic composition of capital; and monopoly.

Harvey himself argues that "product-innovation cycles" may be a counteracting tendency because the early stages of new product production are typically labor-intensive (ibid., 184). He also adds as an "offset" increasing specialization of capitalist firms, which increases efficiency and reduces turnover time of capital (ibid.). Harvey's discussion of the relation between the composition of capital, forms of capitalist organization, technology, and the profit rate is highly enlightening.

processes insofar as capital deploys them to resolve the contradiction between value production and realization and/or to increase the rate of exploitation.[118]

Until recent decades, most if not all neo-orthodox Marxists argued that capital's most powerful "crisis fix" is the expanded reserve army of labor and the reorganization of labor markets, which permit wage cuts, speed-up, and increased labor exploitation. Most Marxists today, however, maintain that the most important form of crisis-induced economic change is the process of restructuring of productive capital, including and especially constant capital (which is not included in *Capital* as an offsetting tendency). Finally, many neo-orthodox theorists stress the importance of the process of state intervention in crisis prevention, management, and resolution, especially with respect to restructuring of constant capital.

It will pay to address these issues one at a time. The first concerns the role of the reserve army of labor, the reorganization of labor markets, and changes in the form of labor power in the crucible of economic bad times. In his writings on the crisis of 1847, Marx stressed the effects of unemployment on increasing competition between workers and its effects on wage determination.[119] In *Capital* he maintained this emphasis on the reserve army of labor, which he described as the "lever of capital accumulation." This means that capitalist economy requires a reserve labor force during periods of economic growth to permit particular branches of the economy to expand "without injury to the scale of production in other spheres."[120] Marx also argued that the reserve army "regulates the wage rate" – that is, it functions to prevent large increases in wage rates during periods of economic expansion.

The question arises, what is the importance of the reserve army during periods of economic crisis and contraction? Does the increase in reserve labor permit wage cuts and speed-up and

---

[118] Bob Catley uses the concept of offsetting tendencies in this latter sense in "Vulgar Marxism," *Arena*, 40 (1975). The majority of neo-orthodox Marxists appear to use the concept in the former sense.

[119] Marx and Engels, *Collected Works*, vol. 6, 430.

[120] Marx, *Capital*, I, 632.

a rise in the rate of exploitation, in this way functioning as a "lever of accumulation"? Many years ago, Maurice Dobb suggested as much when he argued that working-class economic strength during economic booms helps to cause crisis. "From the standpoint of capital, progress is arrested and crises occur because wages are 'too high'."[121] Put briefly, Dobb's position was that the tide that leads to fortune is the ebb tide of crisis and economic contraction which re-creates the reserve army and lowers wages, in this way restoring conditions of profitable accumulation.

Most neo-orthodox Marxists today argue that the reserve army of labor is of secondary importance in the process of crisis-resolution. "The crisis derives from the necessity for a fundamental restructuring of *productive* capital," according to Ben Fine and Laurence Harris.

High ... unemployment does not basically result from the need of distributional struggle (although this plays a secondary, related role), but from the need for a break in the circuit of capital to release money, means of production and labor-power, so that they can, at a later stage of the cycle when the expansion of capital's circuit is renewed, be re-employed in a circuit based on a restructuring of productive capital.[122]

---

[121] "What was to prevent capital accumulation, with the increasing demand for labour which it engendered, from raising the wage-level until surplus-value disappeared, so that capitalism of its own momentum should extinguish the class inequality of which it was reared? ... The crucial factor which operated here – according to Marx's theory, the defensive mechanism by which the system inhibited its own self-extinction – consisted in the double reaction whereby the industrial reserve army was periodically recruited: the tendency of capitalist economy to have a bias towards 'labour-saving' changes and the tendency for accumulation to be retarded and investment to recoil when signs of any appreciable fall in the rate of profit appeared. On the one hand, this intensive recruitment of a labour-reserve ... and, on the other hand, the extensive recruitment of new labour-supplies by increase in population, by proletarianization of intermediate social strata, or by extension of investment in virgin colonial areas, were the factors which operated continually to depress the price of labour-power to a level which permitted surplus-value to be earned. ... From the standpoint of capital, accordingly, progress is arrested and crises occur, because wages are 'too high'.": Maurice Dobb, "Economic crisis," *Political Economy and Capitalism* (London, 1937), 127–8.

[122] Ben Fine and Laurence Harris, "'State expenditure in advanced capi-

According to this argument, crisis reduces the value of constant capital without impairing its physical productivity. The decline in the value composition of capital without a concomitant decrease in its technical composition raises the profit rate. Further, capital restructuring redistributes existing surplus value to fewer capitals, and thereby increases efficiency and the profit rate. The phasing out of inefficient capitals and improvements in the efficiency of surviving capitals occur in two ways. The "normal process" of crisis-induced bankruptcy or business failure reallocates existing surplus value to more productive capitals, hence raising average profitability. The buying up or absorption and cannibalizing of weaker capitals by more productive capitals has a similar effect.

It is also widely argued by neo-orthodox Marxists that capital restructuring today takes the form of the growth of more specialized production units and the fragmentation and relocation of industry on a wider geographical scale. Industrial fragmentation and relocation (or what Harvey calls capital's "spatial fix") raises the average rate of profit in at least three ways. First, the geographic expansion of industry permits capital to exploit a widening circle of reserve labor created by the industrialization of the countryside, or the capitalization of world agriculture. The argument continues that capitalist efficiency increases with the development of the division of social labor – for example, when certain regions specialize in administration, finance, research and development, and related activities, while others specialize in basic or light industry, as well as further specialization of individual production units themselves. Second, capital mobility and industrial relocation inhibit worker migration to older industrial centers; the working class remains divided geographically, and "foreign" workers are prevented from winning access to high wages and social benefits in the older industrial regions. Third, industry typically relocates to countries with authoritarian or militaristic regimes which are eager to help finance new investments and to

talism': a critique," *New Left Review*, 98 (July–August 1976), 112 (italics added).

prevent the development of and/or suppress local workers' movements.

Combining these lines of thought leads to the conclusion that crisis-induced re-creation of the reserve army of labor is a lever of accumulation *to the degree that it is a lever of capital restructuring*. Lay-offs during the first stage of crisis permit capital to re-establish its social and political domination of the working class, which is the precondition for restructuring means of production and relocating industry. In turn, capital concentration and centralization, increases in efficiency, and industrial relocation increase unemployment to higher levels. In subsequent periods of economic expansion, a larger reserve army is thus available to throw into "the battle of production." It is not the original lay-offs but the "second-round" unemployment resulting from capital restructuring that makes the subsequent boom possible without excessive upward pressures on wage rates. In this sense, the reserve army is the key to restructuring the means of production and to the system's capacity to enter into a new phase of economic expansion. This process may be supplemented by the restructuring of the workforce itself through changes in education, labor recruitment, collective-bargaining systems, and welfare which reshape labor power in forms which satisfy new capitalist needs.[123]

The second and related source of economic revival is the increase in the demand for new capital goods (or modernization investments) by consumer- and capital-goods industries desperately attempting to defend sinking profits by cost-cutting innovations. "Instead of capital widening, capital deepening becomes the characteristic feature of the investment process. Or, in other terms, investment primarily does not serve capital expansion but the rationalization of productive processes."[124] While "capital deepening" has a buoyant effect on profits in many if not all industries in the capital-goods sector, it has a weak effect on employment and wages because new investment grows at a

---

[123] David Deitch, "The new capitalist strategy," *The Nation*, November 12, 1973, 498.

[124] Altvater, "The double character of the current crisis of the capitalist world system," 17.

relatively slow rate and also tends to be labor-saving. Moreover, the expansion of "high-tech" capital-goods industries depends on the internationalization of branches of production of these industries, – for example, semi-conductor-based products in the 1970s and 1980s. In the heat of crisis there can be observed increased economic activity in certain capital-goods industries (e.g. micro-electronics today); this is partly explicable in terms of the decline of more established industries (e.g. older smokestack industries), which are compelled to order new innovations and equipment to reduce costs, reimpose control over the labor force, and also relocate internationally as the price of survival in the world market.[125] It is perhaps in this sense more than any other that "capital accumulates through crisis" while keeping large numbers of workers impoverished, and this creates "objective" possibilities for political struggle (see chapter 3).

Economic Crisis and the State

Since World War II, the role of the state in the economy has greatly expanded. "State capitalism," "political capitalism," and "mixed economy" are some of the terms coined to describe new forms of state regulation of the accumulation process. In the past decade or two, Marxist theorists have discussed and debated the significance of state interventionism at great length.[126] A central focus of this discussion has been the role of the state in the creation, prevention, management, and resol-

[125] Conference of Socialist Economists, Microelectronics Groups, *Microelectronics: Capitalist Technology and the Working Class* (London, 1980); "The Economy in Review," *Dollars and Sense*, 11 (November 1975).

A highly sophisticated discussion of the complex links between the development of high technology, capital investment, and industrial relocation today is: Global and Conceptual Studies Branch, Division for Industrial Studies, *Restructuring World Industry in the Period of Crisis – The Role of Innovation: An Analysis of Recent Developments in the Semiconductor Industry*, United Nations Industrial Development Organization, New York, December 17, 1981.

[126] The first political economist in the Marxist tradition to deal systematically with the relationship between capital, finance capital, and the

ution of economic crises. According to some theorists, the accumulation process is not "self-regulating" in the traditional sense, and the capacity of capitalism to secure favorable profit conditions depends increasingly on political means and legitimations and on economic planning.[127] In the contemporary literature, some writers focus on monetary and fiscal policy; others on state subsidies to industry or state-directed industrial reorganization; still others on the restructuring of education, welfare, and other state agencies in ways that promote capital accumulation.[128] There is also a literature on the effects of nationalization of industry, and economic policies which promote the internationalization of production and thus weaken the state's ability to regulate the domestic economy.[129] Further, there have appeared many discussions of the relationship between monopoly capital, economic policy, and "stagflation."[130] Finally, there are countless empirical studies of

---

state was Rudolph Hilferding in *Finance Capital: A Study of the Latest Phase of Capitalist Development*, edited with an introduction by Tom Bottomore (London, 1981). *Finance Capital* was first published in 1910 (Paul Mattick, *Telos*, 54, (Winter 1982–3)). In Mattick's words, Hilferding believed that "the capitalist system not only has no inherent tendency to economic and political crisis, but had transformed itself into an 'organized economy' consciously maintained in equilibrium through state regulation" (ibid., 202). Hilferding advanced a "disproportionality" theory of crisis in which "correct" price structures between and within means of production and means of consumption industries, and financial capital/state planning, would free capitalism from the inevitability of crisis.

[127] The theme of economic planning was developed within the Marxian tradition by the Frankfurt School economists – Friedrich Pollock, Kurt Mandelbaum, and others – who studied the ways in which state planning may prevent or manage crisis.

[128] For example, J. Hirsch, "The state apparatus and social reproduction: elements of a theory of the bourgeois state," in J. Holloway and S. Picciotto (eds), *State and Capital: A Marxist Debate* (London, 1978).

[129] Bergesen states that crisis resolution requires not only private business mergers but "state with firm" mergers, because the state is "the next largest organizational format for production" ("Crisis in the world system: an introduction," 11).

[130] For example, Howard Sherman, *Stagflation* (New York, 1976). There has been much dispute about the effects of monopoly power on prices, hence inflation. A good review is Howard Sherman, "Monopoly power and profit rates," *RRPE*, 15, 2 (Summer 1984).

the role of the state in crisis-resolution in particular countries today. In Japan, for example, the state attempts simultaneously to increase the rate of exploitation, increase aggregate demand by state budgetary policies, and create more flexible monetary controls to prevent a financial collapse.[131] In Italy, policy-makers and capitalists have debated four different strategies: first, the pursuit of the internationalization of production and growth of exports, meanwhile postponing structural reforms at home; second, new forms of authoritarian political rule and the restoration of capital's domination of labor directly in production; third, managed recession to loosen up the labor market; fourth, restructuring of the industrial-relations system and the labor market, and new social reforms to ease social tensions.[132]

A brief review of some of the theoretical literature will suggest to the reader not only the variety of positions taken by neo-orthodox Marxists and others but also the contradictory nature of the state's role in the process of capitalist accumulation through crisis. One line of thought pertains to monetary policy. It has been argued that monetary policy designed to prevent inflation and/or recession by making the money supply more flexible and keeping interest rates down may have the effect of helping to cause either or both.[133] State credit money created to realize fictitious capital values (as well as commodity values which may not otherwise be realized) in effect devalues money. The devaluation of money tends to transform a tendency toward overproduction of capital into inflation.[134]

---

[131] Nagashima, "Business cycles under state monopoly capitalism," 35.

[132] Alberto Martinelli, "Business organized interests and politics: the Italian case," MS, undated, 15–16.

The empirical literature on state initiated crisis resolution in different countries today is so vast that it has not even been summarized, let alone evaluated. Even in England, the "home of political economy," I know of no works which compare and contrast studies such as Glyn and Sutcliffe, *Capitalism in Crisis*; R. Gutman, "State intervention and the economic crisis: the Labour government's economic policy, 1974–1975," *Kapitalistate*, 4–5 (1976); B. Fine and L. Harris, "The British economy, May, 1975–June, 1976," *Bulletin of the Conference of Socialist Economists*, 14 (1976).

[133] Harvey, *The Limits to Capital*, 296.

[134] Ibid., 295.

Another line of argument pertains to the effects of state expenditures and fiscal policy. Some writers hold that the state socializes (i.e. pays for out of taxes) a portion of the costs of constant capital; this prevents the value composition of capital from rising and hence may inhibit the tendency of the rate of profit to fall.[135] On the other hand, state welfare and employment policies have the effect of reducing the rate of exploitation – among other ways, by creating a buffer between the reserve army of labor and the productively employed workforce – thus offsetting the positive effects of the socialization of capital costs on the profit rate.[136] This leads to the conclusion that the rate of exploitation must be increased for capitalism to break out of its impasse, but that the amount of capital investment required to increase relative surplus value (hence the profit rate) is very large and not readily available except at the price of bigger state budgetary deficits and/or more inflated credit structures.

This line of reasoning has been questioned by both "Keynesian Marxists" and neo-orthodox theorists. The former defend the view that military spending or the "permanent arms economy" has been capitalism's important prop in the sense of maintaining aggregate demand or realizing values. According to this view, the only real barriers to economic expansion are political, i.e. ruling-class resistance to redistribution through the expansion of social consumption, which (it is argued) could

---

[135] Paul Walton and Andrew Gamble, *Capitalism and Crisis: Inflation and the State* (London, 1976).

[136] Ian Gough, *The Political Economy of the Welfare State* (London, 1979). In the "crisis of liberal democratic capitalism," the state is not an *"ineffective intervention* into a crisis that is precipitated by the autonomous process of capitalist accumulation," but rather a "site that is *integral to the production* of crisis as well as its resolution": Samuel Bowles and Herbert Gintis, "The crisis of liberal democratic capitalism: the case of the United States," *Politics and Society*, 11, 1 (1982), 60. The authors focus on the adverse effects on profits of rising levels of social services and transfer payments which (they argue) have increased total consumption; this, in turn, has limited possibilities of increasing the rate of exploitation.

A more capital-logic, neo-orthodox view of the welfare state and crisis tendencies is Bennett Harrison, "Welfare payments and the reproduction of low wage workers and secondary jobs," *RRPE*, 11, 2 (Summer 1979), 9.

restore the health of capitalism.[137] Some neo-orthodox Marxists have strengthened this argument with the claim that military spending not only maintains effective demand but also fails to increase the value composition of capital because military equipment and materials are regarded as "luxury goods" which do not enter into the reproduction of labor power or capitalist reproduction as a whole. Paul Boccara has tried to show that the state can counteract the falling profit rate and prevent crises by nationalizing branches of industry which are unprofitable and directly organizing production without, however, sharing in the appropriation of surplus value, thus redistributing a given mass of surplus value over a smaller mass of private capital. These arguments, however, seem to explain the absence of crisis rather than the crisis itself, excepting the tendency toward permanent inflation and/or stagflation. The mainstream of neo-orthodoxy argues that arms spending does, in fact, maintain aggregate demand, but, in the last analysis, utilizes surplus value unproductively. Increasingly less surplus value is available for the increasing requirements of replacing and expanding fixed and circulating constant capital. The limit of the "mixed economy" is the point at which government spending appropriates such a large part of value that there is too little available for continued private capital accumulation.[138]

---

[137] Paul A. Baran and Paul M. Sweezy, *Monopoly Capital* (New York, 1966). It is interesting to note that the official Soviet theory of modern capitalism has been that the state can provide effective "external markets," hence that the threat of underconsumption and economic breakdown is no longer present: Richard Day, *The Crisis and the Crash* (London, 1981), 281–4.

[138] Mattick, *Marx and Keynes: The Limits of the Mixed Economy.* One neo-orthodox writer states that "the ultimate cost of state expenditures falls ... solely on capital.... The provision of state provided use values is not something that has already been paid for by workers through the income tax. It is a tax on capital, which is a drain on the total surplus value produced": Norman Ginsberg, *Class, Capital, and Society Policy* (London, 1979), 26–7.
These arguments neglect the possibility that many if not most state expenditures are socialized forms of capital costs (O'Connor, *The Fiscal Crisis of the State*), and also that arms development may be part and parcel of the development of science and technology (which indirectly helps to valorize private capital) and that technical training of armed personnel has "spillover"

Still another point of contention is related to the state's role in capital restructuring during periods of economic crisis. The traditional argument is that market forces themselves are sufficient to permit capital to reorganize itself during crises. This does not necessarily occur in the ways that Marx himself described, namely, price deflation, especially devaluation of constant capital, which reduces the value composition without affecting the technical composition of capital and thus increases the rate of profit. This version may be unrealistic in a world of monopolies and monopoly control of price[139] (although increased international competition and the internationalization of production arguably makes it more realistic). It may be more plausible to argue that market discipline expresses itself more forcefully via the credit system and stock market. Marx's own view was that credit plays a greater role in crisis-creation (especially in relation to igniting inflation) than crisis-resolution.[140] However, overextension of credit during economic booms results in rising debt/equity ratios, which cause periodic liquidity crises and business failures, hence the concentration and centralization of large and more productive capitals. In this view, the purging of weaker capitals and the redistribution of surplus value to stronger capitals occurs without any need for political intervention. Meanwhile, the

---

value to private capital (James M. Cypher, "A prop, not a burden," *Dollars and Sense* (January 1984)).

[139] "The problem is that we have no reliable analysis of the destruction of capital value or its mechanism. I have thought that under monopoly capitalism the lasting low utilization of capacity still brings about a gradual loss of capital value or a violent destruction of it" (Nagashima, "Business cycles under state monopoly capitalism," 36).

[140] Marx's view was that "credit accelerates the violent eruptions of this contradiction – crises – and thereby the elements of disintegration of the old mode of production. . . . The credit system appears as the main level of over production and over speculation in commerce solely because a larger part of the social capital is employed by people who do not own it and who consequently tackle things quite differently than the owner. . . . This simply demonstrates the fact that the self expansion of capital . . . permits an actual free development only up to a certain point, so that, in fact, it constitutes an immanent fetter and barrier to production, which are continually broken through by the credit systems" (*Capital*, III, 441).

willingness of capitalist and institutional investors to supply money capital only to big capitalist firms appears to be greater during crises: the so-called two-tier stock market tends to starve smaller enterprises seeking funds for modernization or expansion.[141] The resulting "passive destruction" of inefficient capitals raises average efficiency and the average rate of profit in the economy as a whole. On the other hand, the counter-argument is that the state is needed actively to intervene in the process of capital restructuring, however inefficiently it does so.[142] Selective tariffs and subsidies, research and development in fields such as energy exploitation and utilization, and similar policies, selectively deflate capital values and destroy smaller and/or weaker capitals. Policies deliberately designed to reduce inflation rates by creating recessions and unemployment have the same effect. On the other hand, it has been maintained that "bureaucratic innovation and restructuring is a less vigorous and less viable process of evolving new forms of capitalism than the 'free market' version."[143] This may be true in "special-interest"-dominated countries such as the USA, where "reprivatization" of social services has proved to be a boon to private capital, and less true in more "collectivist" countries such as Japan.

In sum, there is considerable disagreement about the effects of state interventionism on economic crisis tendencies. Each line of analysis begins with different premises regarding the effects of state credit and/or spending on aggregate demand, the

[141] 'Can US industry find the money it needs," *Business Week*, September 22, 1973.

[142] David Yaffe has argued that the state can do little else except to promote capital restructuring (and raise the rate of exploitation) to restore good profit conditions: "The Marxian theory of crisis, capital, and the state," *Economy and Society*, 2, 2 (1973).

[143] Harvey, *The Limits to Capital*, 328. A convincing and extreme variation of this view has been argued by André Gundar Frank, who write that, "if we recall what happened with the present world crisis, we were a long way into the ... crisis before any of these leaders – West, East and South – even recognized where they were, let alone formulating any kind of policy to get us out of it" ("Policy ad hockery: unemployment and world crisis of economic policy formation," paper delivered at Round Table '83, Marxism and the World Today, Cavtat, Yugoslavia, (October 24–8, 1983, 15).

composition of capital, the costs of capital, the rate of exploitation, and so on. Hence, each tends to draw different and often
contradictory conclusions. Further, there is little discussion of
the possibility that politicians and state planners may use the
world "crisis" ideologically. "Talk of 'crisis,'" John Keane
writes, "can easily become valuable material in the hands of the
political technicians"[144] because "crisis" in this sense is associated not with social struggles and transformation but with the
actions of the ruling class and power elite directing the economy
in the name of rationality and common interests to do whatever
is required to strengthen themselves and their power.[145] This
meaning of "crisis," Touraine writes, "is not a situation but an
incapacity to act."[146]

   Also, most if not all neo-orthodox Marxists (not to speak of
"Keynesian Marxists") neglect the crucial issues of the rise of
the state bureaucracy and the administration of society, as well
as the relation between the social conditions of reproduction of
labor power and the working class and salariat and economic
crisis.[147] Finally, most if not all neo-orthodox and "revisionist"
Marxist theories of capital and the state neglect not only the
process whereby capitalist crisis tendencies are displaced into
the state budget[148] and bureaucracy itself, but also the way in
which class struggle is similarly displaced – that is, the way in
which class struggle assumes the form of struggles within and
against the capitalist state form.

---

[144] John Keane, "Crisis in the industrial world?", *Canadian Journal of
Political Science Theory*, 3, 2 (Spring–Summer 1979), 183.
   [145] Alain Touraine, "Crisis or transformation?", in Norman Birnbaum
(ed.), *Beyond the Crisis* (New York, 1977). "Crisis tendencies are most often a
condition of renewal of the existing order. As both Marx and Burckhardt
forcefully pointed out in the nineteenth century, crises may allow the
unilateral, authoritarian abolition of a host of practises from which it is
deemed life has long since departed" (Keane, "Crisis in the industrial world?"
188); "The productivity slowdown," *Dollars and Sense* (September 1981),
12.
   [146] Touraine, "Crisis or transformation?", 45.
   [147] An analysis of this issue may be found in O'Connor, *Accumulation
Crisis*, chapter 7.
   [148] This is one subject of O'Connor, *The Fiscal Crisis of the State*.

Conclusion

Such are the results of the revival of Marxist economic orthodoxy and its applications to contemporary capitalism, as well
as of "class struggle" crisis theory. The latent scientism of the
former leads most if not all neo-orthodox Marxists theoretically
to render the world silent and colorless, peopled by abstractions, a kind of social laboratory. The "economy" remains a
separate "system" (and, in the post-Marxist world of writers
such as Jürgen Habermas, a "sub-system"), the understanding
of which (it is thought) may be safely abstracted from culture
and society, ideologies of social domination, and contradictions
inherent in modern personality structures. In this pre-
Gramscian and pre-Freudian world, social groups and classes
engaged in struggles for survival and emancipation come to life
on the historical stage during the second act of the drama
("social and political crisis") upon completion of the first act
("economic crisis"), in which individuals and groups are seen as
little more than movable stage props. More concrete, but not
necessarily mutually exclusive, theories are presented in the
next chapter, where it is argued that social groups and classes,
human intersubjectivity, and personality structures themselves
are constituent causes as well as effects of "economic crisis."
This perspective escapes neo-orthodox Marxism and also "Keynesian Marxism," albeit not certain neo-Marxist and "class
struggle" crisis theorists, whose thought, however, is limited by
the Hegelian–Marxist method based on the "identity principle"
and their failure adequately to distinguish the economic, social,
and personal spheres of existence, hence their inability to grasp
the ways in which these spheres interpenetrate and potentially
negate one another.

3

Social and Political Crisis Theory

Introduction

The classical definition of "crisis" is the turning point of an illness "in which it is decided whether or not the organism's self-healing powers are sufficient for recovery." In traditional Marxist economic theory, the word has been used in roughly analogous ways for a century or more ("economic crisis," as well as "moral crisis" and "spiritual crisis" were common as early as the seventeenth century, but their meanings were vague and their status in social and political thought was weak). In late eighteenth-century political discourse, "crisis" also assumed familiar meanings – "time for decision" and "political transformation." A good example is Thomas Paine's *The American Crisis* published in 1776. A century later, "crisis" was associated with the trials and tribulations of nation-building and the expansion of empire. Historians came to use the word to mean "critical moments when national character and institutions were thought to have been decisively tested."[1]

In the twentieth century, with the triumph of positivistic social science, more objectivist concepts appeared, such as "an historical crisis is a dynamic state, but it differs from a dynamic equilibrium in exhibiting uncoordinated rather than coordinate development. When there is a grievous disturbance of equilib-

---

[1] Randolf Stern, "Historians and crisis," *Past and Present*, 52 (August 1971), 9.

108

rium, producing a terrifying acceleration of the historical process, and little coordination among societal elements, there is a genuine crisis."[2] This view is not very different from Jacob Burckhardt's classical definition of crisis as a massive and uncontrolled transformation of society insofar as this transformation is "genuine" – a rare occurrence, in Burckhardt's opinion. These and related meanings have been widely used in the twentieth century to describe imperialist rivalries and world wars; national liberation struggles and counter-revolutions; dangerous moments in the Cold War; the transformation of race relations; the "break-up" of the modern family, and so on. "Social crisis" and "political crisis" have been loosely applied to these and other events and processes which hindsight may or may not reveal to have been "crises" in any traditional sense of the word.

Precise definitions of social and political crisis are hard to find in the orthodox Marxist, neo-Marxist, or mainstream literature. Social crisis has been associated with class and social struggles; disintegration of educational, judicial, and other social institutions; mass anomie; and social and/or cultural revolution. Political crisis has been associated with sharp turns to the political right or left; a polarization of attitudes towards the capitalist state or political system; mass discontent with bourgeois democratic norms; and political revolution.[3] However, the most common concept of political crisis revolves around the concept of "legitimation," a word which has a

---

[2] Melvin Rader, *Marx's Interpretation of History* (New York, 1979), 190.

[3] Ekkart Zimmermann provides a brief review of some of the leading concepts of "political crisis," including "government collapse": "The study of crisis in liberal democracies: pitfalls and promises," *International Political Science Review*, 5, 3 (1984), 325. His own definition is "crises of the political system, as political crises that are conceived in a wider sense than mere government crises, cabinet crises, or coalition crises. Political crises more or less call for and possibly lead to *substantial* changes in policies or the political order, not to a mere replacement of personnel" (ibid., 320). "Political crisis" remains an amorphous concept in a most interesting attempt to deduce political tendencies, constituencies for leftist strategies, and crisis solutions from different Marxist and semi- and quasi-Marxist economic crisis theories: Val Burris, "The politics of Marxist crisis theory," *Research in Political Economy*, vol. 7 (Greenwich, Conn., 1984).

bewildering variety of meanings in bourgeois thought.[4] In orthodox Marxism, however, the concepts of legitimation and "legitimation crisis" have no status whatsoever. "Marxian analysis does not assume that the liberal capitalist state is based on mass legitimacy" but rather that its stability depends "on the ideological consensus among the ruling groups plus mass acquiescence by the underclass to the routine demands imposed by the institutions created in the name of that ideology."[5] By contrast, in neo-Marxist theory, legitimation crisis (a "loyalty deficit") is defined as a strong tendency for the political system or state bureaucracy to cease to work, which may or may not be accompanied by popular political opposition. Political crisis in this sense is the incapacity of the political system or state to function normally and/or inspire sufficient belief or loyalty. More specifically, legitimation depends on the capacity of the political system to secure a consensus of political policies from groups which either will not benefit or will be harmed by

---

[4] The central role of the concept in bourgeois thought derives from Max Weber's discussion of the conditions of legitimate authority, which includes competent politicians and bureaucrats, rational planning, and so on. It also derives from Durkheim's work which (to use the modern concept) stresses the importance of "normative integration," which Marxists regard as a code word for the internalization of oppression by oppressed classes and groups. As one writer puts it, "in advanced Western industrial societies ... there are manifold notions of legitimacy that citizens and politicians hold and try to act upon. Legitimacy thus is a plural concept" (Zimmermann, "The study of crises in liberal democracies," 325). According to another writer, "there are two major viewpoints about the cause of crisis in the liberal capitalist state. The conventional pluralist view is that the loss of mass based legitimacy or support is critical to the political system. This view holds that the liberal pluralistic state is supported and held together by social consensus on the rules of the game. The democratic elitist version ... stresses the necessity of consensus among political activists or the political elite on the rules of the game as a necessary condition for political stability": Edward Malecki, "Public opinion, socialization, and ideology from a Marxian perspective," MS, undated, 6–7. According to yet another writer, moral, ideological, and functional types of legitimation crisis are possible – pertaining to disillusionment with a political regime, the core values of the system, and workability of public institutions, respectively: Daniel Yankelovich, *New Rules: Searching for Self-Fulfillment in a World Turned Upside Down* (New York, 1981).

[5] Malecki, "Public opinion, socialization, and ideology from a Marxian perspective," 7.

capitalist accumulation – a task which typically requires that policies be defined and presented to the "public" in ways that conceal their true nature. As we shall see, the capacity to secure consensus is threatened when political parties and politicians who make claims that they are able to manage capitalism and accumulation successfully cannot in fact do so. In this way, the idea of political legitimation is tied to the capacity of the state bureaucracy to reproduce legitimating ideologies and also successfully to implement crisis-prevention or crisis-management policies.

The difference between orthodox and neo-Marxist approaches to the problem of political crisis in general and legitimation in particular is doubtless explicable in terms of the transformation of the class structure since the heyday of classical capitalism. In Marx's day, the working class was undeveloped and in times of trouble simply repressed. The main problems of political legitimation concerned rivalries between and within fractions of the propertied classes. By contrast, the working class has reached its political majority in modern capitalism. It is therefore reasonable to assume that the problem of legitimation exists precisely because a majority of propertyless citizens exercise bourgeois democratic rights enshrined in constitutions established by propertied minorities.

Traditional Marxist Theories of Social Crisis

Marx revolutionized the tradition of nineteenth-century economic crisis theory with such force and clarity that the conventions which he established are retained today as the beginning (and, often, the end) of modern discussions of economic crisis. He also inherited the nineteenth-century historian's convention of defining crisis in terms of social upheaval and political revolution and counter-revolution. However, unlike the majority of nineteenth-century writers, he conceived of social unrest and revolution not only in terms of bourgeois revolutions against the old order and European nationalism and anti-imperialism, but also in terms of working-class revolution against the domination of the bourgeoisie. Marx used the word "crisis" primarily in his political economy theory, and he rarely conceived of working-class revolution actually occurring in his own time in any other context than a successful or failed bourgeois revolution (in the former case, the workers might successfully push the revolution beyond the point which the bourgeoisie itself regarded as desirable; in the latter case, the workers might replace bourgeois with proletarian demands after first completing the "bourgeois stage" themselves). However, as early as 1847 he linked the "uproar" of the workers to the economic crisis which crashed upon Europe that year, suggesting that governments would be compelled to grant "important reforms."[6] In the same year, Engels anatomized the bourgeois revolution in Germany, its relation to the economic crisis, and the reaction of the old ruling classes.[7] For Marx and Engels, however, social and political crises were not primarily identified with struggles between and within national bourgeoisies, landed classes, etc. (as they were by late eighteen- and early nineteenth-century writers), but rather with the class struggle between capital and labor. "Crisis" was the turning point not only in the unpredictable and chaotic process of bourgeois revolution, but also in relation to the political class struggle between capital and labor. In the nineteenth century, crisis as "transformation" meant, first, bourgeois revolution and counter-revolution and, secondly, the working-class revolution against capitalism.

In Marx's view, every economic crisis is by definition conjunctural, and crisis-induced capital restructuring is never certain to restore the domination of capital over labor and profitable conditions of accumulation. National capital's own self-healing powers may be too weak in relation to capital based in rival countries. More important, capital restructuring is a qualitative as well as quantitative process; crises are "turning points" in the process of social reproduction as a whole. Hence economic crises were thought to be closely associated with social crises and social movements, and struggles by the

[6] Karl Marx and Frederick Engels, *Collected Works*, vol. 6 (New York, 1976), 305.
[7] Ibid., 69.

"proletarian army" which militarily rebels against the class dictatorship of the capitalist state. Engels created the vision of "poorly armed swarms of petty bourgeoisie," "heavy artillery of capital," "closed-columns of its joint-stock companies," and "long files of proletariat" in one of his writings on the crisis of 1847.[8] Crises became cauldrons not only for capital restructuring in the economic and material sense but also for the rise of reformist, utopian, revolutionary, and counter-revolutionary movements, including (in twentieth-century Marxism) fascism and other extreme kinds of social and political restructuring.[9] In brief, it is implicit in both orthodox and neo-Marxist writings that capitalism is not merely subject to political crises; crises are also the cauldrons in which new political formations are born and develop in the context of changes in the composition of social classes and class, national, and other struggles.

A necessary but not sufficient condition for proletarian revolution (it was thought) was that the hardships of economic crisis – unemployment, poverty, devaluation of capital values, and so on – undermine the hegemonic ideology of capitalist society, namely, commodity and capital fetishism. "Crisis entailed the explosion of the ideology of equal exchange of equivalents; the productive powers which are the property of labor no longer appear as capital. Rather, the productive powers and properties of capital and labor stand in open opposition."[10] This approach underscores the contingent and

[8] Ibid., 82. It may be added that Marx and Engels's *Correspondence* is replete with military metaphors for social and class struggles.

[9] Peter R. Sinclair, "Fascism and crisis in capitalist society," *New German Critique*, 9 (Fall 1976); Burris, "The politics of Marxist crisis theory." Historically, political reactions to economic crisis have taken a wide variety of forms depending on the class structure, political systems, and so on, in particular countries: Ekkart Zimmermann, "The 1930s world economic crisis in six European countries: a first report on causes of political instability and reactions to crisis," in Paul M. Johnson and William R. Thompson (eds), *Rhythms in Politics and Economics* (New York, 1985). Today there are a variety of political responses to the modern economic crisis, e.g. moderation of wage demands coupled with investment plans to increase productivity and/or worker participation in management; rationalization of national capitalism to compete more effectively on the world market; reform of social institutions designed to take the political bite out of mass youth unemploy-

unpredictable nature of historical moments when capital loses its "normal ideological sovereignty," hence when there may occur a political vacuum in which political power is up for grabs. Traditional Marxism thus modifies the medical model of crisis, raising possibilities not only of a restoration of capital's normal powers but also of revolutionary social and political transformation. As John Keane shows, this perspective owes a big debt to the "tradition of tragic theater, in which the perilous moment of crisis is eternal," a tradition that exemplifies this sense of crisis as "moments which present rich possibilities for the regaining of free subjectivity against the pseudo-power of Fate."[11]

There are two possible traditional or neo-orthodox interpretations of the relationship between economic and social crisis. The first and most popular is that economic crisis directly causes social crisis – that social disintegration and political class struggle presuppose the disintegration of the economic system. The second and least theoretically developed within traditional Marxism is that economic and social crises are simultaneous processes which have a common cause.

According to the first view, which deserves to be expounded at some length, capital develops according to its own inner logic or laws of motion, and economic crisis or breakdown creates both the possibility and the need for social and political revolution. This idea is partly rooted in the messianic tradition in which redemption comes only during periods of total corrup-

---

ment; above all, neo-liberalism and neo-conservatism. Some relevant studies are Ernest Mandel, *The Second Slump* (London, 1978); Walter Korpi, *The Working Class in Welfare Capitalism* (London, 1978); Samuel Bowles, David Gordon and Thomas Weisskopf, *Free Lunch: A Democratic Alternative to the Politics of Greed* (New York, 1983).

[10] Robert Marotto, memo to the author.

[11] John Keane, "Crisis in the industrial world?", *Canadian Journal of Political Science Theory*, 3, 2 (Spring–Summer 1979), 184–5. Keane adds that in Rousseau's thought crisis "raises the possibility that man can be re-made in the image of their true selves" (ibid., 185). Rader recalls that "Marx's knowledge of Greek and Elizabethan plays, when combined with Hegel's dialectical interpretation of comedy and tragedy, must have influenced his interpretation of historical crisis" (*Marx's Interpretation of History*, 194).

tion (after all, crisis and breakdown may lead to apathy and fatalism alone).[12] It is also rooted in the real conditions of nineteenth-century society, when capitalism had not yet established its modern institutional and international forms, hence when the political and ideological weapons of the bourgeoisie, not only of the proletariat, were primitive and unreliable. This idea was first advanced by Marx and Engels themselves, revised by Karl Kautsky[13] and German social democracy, and refined by Lenin and the Bolsheviks. It is kept alive today by neo-orthodox Marxists such as Ernest Mandel, who "makes a fairly sharp separation between the economic dynamics of capitalist economies and the political impact of tendencies and shifts in the force of 'class struggle.'"[14] It is also kept alive by "world system" theorists who argue that international political crises, including shifts in the hegemony of nation-states in world

[12] The idea that social transformation is possible (and in extreme versions inevitable) during massive crises and periods of corruption has a profoundly Christian, millenarianist basis. For example, one of the "central affirmations of the prophets and the early theologians [was that] the decline and fall of empire can become the occasion for the emergence of new and more human social order": Richard Shaull, "Christian faith and the crisis of empire," *Monthly Review* (April 1984), 38.

[13] "The history of mankind is determined, not by the ideas of man, but by the economic development which precedes irresistibly obedient to certain underlying laws and not according to the whims and wishes of people": Karl Kautsky, *The Socialist Republic* (New York, 1904), 34.

[14] David Gordon, "Nowhere to go but down," *The Nation*, April 21, 1979, 438, citing Mandel, *The Second Slump*.

It is worth quoting Ben Fine's lucid statment of the neo-orthodox view in full: "Capitalism will be in or on the verge of crisis whenever the social accumulation of capital is interrupted. In such a circumstance the working class will be posed with two alternatives. It may concede an economic, political or social defeat to restore capital to its normal condition of reproduction on an extended scale. This could, for example, involve a fall in wages or employment, the fighting of a war, or an unpheaval in working conditions. Alternatively the working class can overthrow the system of capitalist production. Marx believed that crises were endemic to capitalism, and in this sense alone revolution against capital was inevitable. For, again and again, the working class would take defeat, but with the lesson of defeat and its growing strength and organization defeat would eventually be inflicted on the *bourgeoisie* at the hands of the proletariat": Ben Fine, *Marx's Capital* (London, 1975), 51.

politics, come about because of international economic changes in general and national economic crisis in particular.[15] This perspective was long ago exemplified by Marx's judgment in the early 1850s that "in view of the general prosperity which now prevails there can be no question of any real revolution. A new revolution will be made possible only as a result of a new crisis."[16]

More than half a century later, Lenin faced a situation in Russia where capitalism was undeveloped, and the Tsar and national and foreign capital blocked both political and economic reforms (and where an aging Marx strongly believed that socialist revolution was possible). The failure of the European working class to make a revolution in the cauldrons of bourgeois democratic movements and political revolutions had brought to the surface the crucial problem of proletarian "subjectivity." No longer was it thought that the breakdown of the normal process of "equal exchange of equivalents" in the course of economic bad times was sufficient to make capitalist workers into a revolutionary proletariat. In Leninist doctrine, workers are condemned to a trade-union consciousness without the active and outside intervention of professional revolutionaries and a democratic centralist party. The crucial point was made that "subjective processes" of working-class consciousness and will-formation are important only insofar as economic crisis creates mass militancy, which becomes the social raw material processed by the party in its efforts to challenge the state. In this view, economic crisis itself remains an objective, external form, while the party organizes and embodies working-class resistance and subjectivity. The party supplies the theoretical analysis of capitalist economy and society, "reforms consciousness," and organizes and leads revolutionary political struggle. In sum, with the slogan

---

[15] Albert Bergesen, "Crisis in the world-system: an introduction," in Albert Bergesen (ed.), *Crisis in the World-System* (Beverly Hills, Cal., 1983).
[16] It is true that Marx was referring to bourgeois political revolution, which was unlikely to occur in good times; in his writings on Germany, proletarian revolution comes only with the failure of bourgeois revolution or its success together with its refusal to "go all the way."

"politics first," the party intervenes in historical processes which otherwise work themselves out in ways which permit capital to re-create conditions for renewed capitalist accumulation.

The idea that economic crisis is "historical objectivity" and the party is "organized subjectivity" may be judged plausible in an epoch when the working class was undeveloped and when the destruction of the three great European empires during World War I created a huge political vacuum. The backwardness of Russia and the chaotic conditions during and after World War I created political spaces for an iron-willed "parent-surrogate" party which could discipline an otherwise anarchic or utopian working class which retained strong traces of the traditional individual and group values of the peasantry, small producer, and craft worker. However, as has been pointed out by many critical theorists and neo-Marxists, the Marxists-Leninist model of economic crisis, consciousness, party, and revolution is both deterministic and voluntaristic. "Hypostatizing objective laws and structures," Paul Breines writes, "is accompanied by a notion of pure subjectivity and voluntarism."[17] Voluntarism, in fact, presupposes determinism in the same sense that "psychological science" presupposes positivistic economic, sociology, and other social sciences. The Marxist-Leninist model suffers from voluntarism because it provides no theory of "historical conjunctures" which permits the party to grasp "real as opposed to imaginary revolutionary possibilities" – Lenin's success notwithstanding.[18] This failure is partly rooted in the (doubtless necessary) lack of historical

[17] Paul Breines, "Towards an uncertain Marxism," *Radical History Review*, 22 (Winter 1979–80), 114, summarizing M. Ponty's arguments.
[18] Peter Beilharz, "Trotsky's Marxism – a permanent revolution?", *Telos*, 39 (Spring 1979). The problem of "voluntarism" was doubtless the main factor giving rise to the theory of economic breakdown or collapse, which Rosa Luxemburg considered to be the "cornerstone of scientific socialism." Without economic crisis and ultimate capitalist breakdown, socialism "ceases to be objectively necessary." As has been often pointed out, there are definite religious aspects to this kind of thinking. The theory itself is supposedly scientific insofar as it discovered and obeyed historical laws; it is religious in the sense that communists accepted these laws on faith. "Some say the writings of Rosa Luxemburg will evoke the same kind of devotion as those of

perspective on the contradictory nature of worker struggles in the past and the problem of the composition and recomposition of the working class through economic crises.[19] This is at least one reason that Leninists make one deterministic connection between crisis and consciousness, and a second between consciousness and party-building. In periods of mass unemployment and impoverishment, it is assumed that "the proletariat could only realize their immediate interests by abandoning them and struggling for their real interests, the abolition of capitalist production relations."[20] In the words of another writer, in bad times, "when the worker comprehends that under capitalist production he is degraded to the status of a mere object, of a commodity, he ceases to be a commodity, an object, and becomes a subject."[21]

The claim that during times of material hardship workers transform themselves from a "heap" of individuals who objectify their labor power to a political class struggling to abolish wage labor as such has posed the most difficult problem that Western Marxism and neo-Marxism has had to try to solve. Marxist theory "is completely dominated by the question of the relation between the crisis and the emergence of revolutionary subjectivity."[22] How do workers know that they can fulfill their needs only by abandoning their immediate economic struggles for revolutionary political action? As we have noted, one "solution" was provided by Marx himself – that crisis destroys the ideology of "equal exchange of equivalents" which is the glue that holds capitalist class society together. This was, however, unsatisfactory. The reason is that traditional Marxism "largely ignored the inward dialectic. . . . it has been quick to recognize the crisis of institutions and slow to recognize the crisis of the human person."[23]

Saint Theresa of Avila": José Mariótiegui, quoted in John Baines, *Revolution in Peru: Mariaatiegui and the Myth* (University [of Alabama], 1972), 110.

[19] James O'Connor, *Accumulation Crisis* (Oxford, 1984), chapter 2.

[20] Review of Herbert Marcuse, *Counter-Revolution and Revolt* (Boston, Mass., 1972), *Telos*, 13 (Fall 1972), 149.

[21] Shlomo Avineri, *The Social and Political Thought of Karl Marx* (London, 1968), 148.

[22] Toni Negri, *Marx Beyond Marx* (South Hadley, Mass., 1984), 11.

[23] Rader, *Marx's Interpretation of History*, 205.

In the early 1920s, the founders of "Western Marxism" – Karl Korsch, Georg Lukács, Antonio Gramsci, and others – sought in their own ways a solution to the problem of working-class consciousness. When they capitalized on the clues to be found in Marx's own words, their solutions became indispensable first approximations to the problem of the development (or lack of it) of revolutionary consciousness. But these solutions were flawed in ways which need to be discussed, however briefly, if only because they (together with the practical failure of revolutionary movements in the 1920s) have had great philosophical and political importance in the West. On the one hand, they helped to inspire modern existentialism and its preoccuption with inner life and personality; on the other hand, they helped to underwrite modern Marxist structuralism (and by extension post-structuralism) and its dismissal of "meaning" and "intentionality."

All of the founders of Western Marxism tried to penetrate the relationship between capitalist social existence and ideology as the key which might solve the problem of the relationship between the crisis of human consciousness and the human consciousness of crisis. Korsch's solution began with the premise that the separation of theoretical Marxism and the working class had been characteristic of Marxism from the beginning. His attempt to discover the determinants of working-class consciousness lay in his analysis of the relationship between bourgeois thought, bourgeois society, and Marxist theory itself. His argument was that a basic condition for the accumulation of capital and the reproduction of capitalism was the popular and general acceptance of "pre-scientific and bourgeois-scientific consciousness."[24] In this view, capitalist relations of production and capitalist society itself cannot exist without hegemonic pre-capitalist and/or capitalist thought. According to Korsch, dialectical Marxism is characterized by the "coincidence of consciousness and reality," and the "major component of a theory of social revolution" is the Marxist critique of science and consciousness. By laying bare the reality

[24] Karl Korsch, *Marxism and Philosophy* (London, 1970), 78.

of capitalist exploitation and destroying bourgeois truths, Marxist theory creates a rupture between reality and consciousness, and hence permits changes in real social processes and material production. In this way, Korsch tried to explain the failure of the worker revolutions through the early 1920s with the claim that it was impossible for the working-class movement to assimilate Marxist theory because of the disjuncture between the theory itself, which was based on mid-nineteenth-century working-class practice, and late-nineteenth-century and early twentieth-century proletarian struggles. In sum, for Korsch the problem was resolved when there was a correct "fit" between Marxist theory and working-class practice. How such a fit could be made; whether theory adjusts to practice or vice versa; what are appropriate forms of political organization – these and related questions remained unanswered. Korsch's positive contribution was to take up the relation between class practices and Marxist theory itself, although his analysis was limited to attempting to explain disjunctures between them. His work leads in the direction of historicizing Marxist theory, which was no small accomplishment, but it neglects or ignores the crucial subject of the historical transformation of working-class composition through economic crises, or class defined in terms of both the global development of capital and the law of value, on the one hand, and forms of class struggle, on the other.

Georg Lukács also stressed the importance of the "reform of consciousness" with his thesis that the working class adopts a revolutionary class consciousness only when workers become conscious of their actual material and social activity and its results. This kind of consciousness, however, does not occur spontaneously. Commodity fetishism is too pervasive and the reification of social life too totalizing. Certain that reform is more difficult during crisis periods because "the crisis-ridden condition of capitalism makes it increasingly difficult to relieve the pressure from the proletariat by making minute concessions," Lukács was equally certain that an "ideological crisis of the proletariat . . . manifests itself in the fact that the objectively extremely precarious position of bourgeois society is endowed in the minds of the workers with all its erstwhile stability and in many respects the proletariat is still caught up in old capitalist forms of thought and feeling."[25] The solution was – the party, whose task was not only to lead the workers' struggle politically, but also to develop and disseminate the theory of capitalist reification and crisis. The subjective conditions for revolutionary proletarian consciousness thus depend not only on party-building but also on the development and dissemination of Marx's critique of capital (the objective conditions for revolutionary consciousness were the hardships of economic crisis which inspired an upsurge of spontaneous protest by the masses). In Eric Hobsbawm's words, "structure and situation interact, and determine the limits of decision and action; but what determines the possibilities of action is the primary situation. At this point the analysis of forces capable of mobilizing, organizing, and moving into action groups of people on a politically decisive scale (e.g. the Leninist Party) becomes relevant."[26]

Western Marxism raised the problem of consciousness and revolution in the early twentieth century in other, albeit related, ways. Anton Pannekoek and Herman Gorter (leading Dutch Council Communists) explained the failure of the rebellions of the 1920s not in terms of "wrong" objective conditions, or disjunctures between Marxist theory and worker practise, or even the failure of the Communist Party to spread Marx's critique of capitalist ideology, but rather because of the dependence of the working class on pre-bourgeois institutions – schools, family, church, and so on. It was Antonio Gramsci, however, who developed most profoundly the idea of bourgeois ideological hegemony and the problems posed for the working-class movement. His strategic political idea is summarized by a leading Gramsci scholar thus: "Any crisis of the established order which might open the way to revolutionary transformation must follow a crisis of ideological hegemony in civil society."[27] This idea remains an indispensable tool of modern

[25] Georg Lukács, *History and Class Consciousness: Studies in Marxist Dialectics* (Cambridge, Mass., 1971), 310.
[26] Eric Hobsbawm, *Revolution*, XIV International Congress of Historical Sciences, San Francisco, August 22–9, 1975, 12.
[27] Carl Boggs, *Gramsci's Marxism* (London, 1976), 40.

revolutionary and reformist practice in the developed and third world countries.[28] It also evolved into the concept of "prefigurative practice," or attempts to develop cooperative and nonhierarchical practices within and against established bourgeois institutions. This idea is consistent with Lukács's (temporary) judgment that all bourgeois institutions should be boycotted because active participation would reproduce reified bourgeois thought and sensibilities within the working class. In the thought of other revolutionaries, it led to the extreme view that workers needed to engage in participatory struggles not only in the workplace, community, groups, and cultural organizations, but also within the Leninist vanguard party itself. Gramsci's contribution has been developed into elaborated forms of criticism/self-criticism and struggles against racism, sexism, national chauvinism, elitism, and individualism in popular movements today. Gramsci's "solution," however, did not and could not address the historical relationship between the development of Marxist theory, bourgeois ideology, and working-class practice – the question Korsch faced but failed adequately to answer at the level of either epistemology or political method. The conceptual links between actual popular critical and prefigurative practice, Marxist theory, and bourgeois ideology remain to this day to be forged.

As we have seen, the first and traditional interpretation of the relationship between economic and social/political crisis is that the former causes the latter. There is a second view, however, which remains well within the boundaries of traditional Marxism – namely, that economic and social crisis spring from a common source. This view has little currency in political circles, doubtless because it does not address directly the question of reform and revolution. However, in one sense, it is more important than the first interpretation because it reveals why crisis theory lies at the heart of Marxism, which many regard as

[28] A "crisis of ideological hegemony" in the USA may develop on the basis of the contradiction between the identification of the American nation with individualism, on the one hand, and the self-destruction of ideologies of individualism through economic and social crisis, on the other (O'Connor, *Accumulation Crisis*).

first and foremost a critique of bourgeois ideology. Economic crisis is central in Marx's thought, not merely because it is seen as the way capitalism helps to subvert itself in fact, but also because crisis is the self-destruction of the two main ideologies which function as capital's historical critique of socialism – an issue which the founders of Western Marxism apparently did not raise. Capital's first and basic ideology is that without individual private property there can be no sustained wealth production ("industry and rationality," in Locke's words). No individual private property, no economic motivations and incentives, much poverty and misery – so goes the chain of reasoning. Marx countered this view with the theory of capital overproduction, falling rate of profit, and economic crisis, which destroys capitalism's own self-justification, as well as one basis of its critique of socialism.

Capital's second critique of socialism is that social stability also presupposes private property. No private property, no propertied middle class, no social order – such is the tradition rationale for private ownership of the means of production (one which dates to Aristotle's *Politics*). Marx in effect countered this view with the theory of the rising composition of capital, capital concentration and centralization, and overproduction, which bring about not only economic crisis but also social crisis – namely, the bankruptcy of the old middle classes and small business – which in turn destroys capitalism's own social self-justification as well as the other basis of its critique of socialism. "Proletarianization through crisis" results in economic poverty *and* social distress; crisis disrupts the process of sustained wealth production *and* social stability, and hence subverts the traditional capitalist critique of socialism.[29]

[29] This is doubtless why (for example) Italian ruling parties in the 1950s tried to strengthen the middle class as an agency of social stabilization and custodian of the status quo; French governments are famous for catering to the demands of the petty bourgeoisie; the German state keeps small business alive under protective price umbrellas; and the USA in the 1930s went to great lengths to protect the petty bourgeoisie. The problem arises, however, that the stabilization of the old middle class to legitimate and maintain the political system is inefficient, hence costly economically.

There is one problem with this formulation of the relationship between capitalist development, economic and social crisis, and ideological hegemony. It interprets capitalism's ideologically self-destructive nature in purely capitalist not socialist terms. During economic crises, private property defined as the production of commodity wealth turns into its opposite – economic depression. This is clearly a capitalist self-critique in terms of exchange-value, not of use-value, production. Moreover, in an economic crisis, private property defined as social stability turns into *its* opposite – social disorder associated with new social inequalities and distress. Not only does the aggregate of produced commodity values decline, but also the distribution of values becomes more unequal or polarized. Neither economic depression nor social disorder, defined in these ways, functions as a socialist critique of capitalist social domination, commodity and capital fetishism, and the wage and commodity forms of work and life.

Neo-Marxist Theories of Social Crisis

Contemporary historiography, social theory, and late capitalist development itself, including the emergence of new social movements and forms of class struggle, have conspired to weaken traditional Marxist concepts of crisis and consciousness, rebellion and party organization, reform and revolution – at least in the developed countries.[30] In the most developed capitalist society, the USA, traditional cultural practices within the working class have been transformed into mass-produced and mass-consumed ideologies of individualism – the myth of the "self" and "self-realization." Similarly, capitalist development has transformed the meaning of "crisis" (which was traditionally defined in separate economic, social,

---

[30] "Crisis theory" traditionally defined has not dealt systematically with the complex combinations of class, national, regional, race, ethnic, and religious struggles in the Third World (a subject which is well beyond the scope of the present work). However, it was doubtless the international debt and economic crisis which underwrote the social turmoil and explosive "IMF riots" of the 1980s, and the growth of a vicious cycle of militarism in both the Third World and the USA.

and political terms) into various crisis ideologies as well as a single and universal historical phenomenon which needs to be understood simultaneously in economic, social, and psychological terms. "Crisis" defined ideologically may be regarded as part of capital's .counter-attack against the working-class offensive against the law of value, including commodity and capital fetishism and social reification in all of its forms. The word is ideological when it is inappropriately substituted for the concept of social transformation of the administrative-technical apparatus of the state by social movements seeking forms of self-management and democracy.[31] "Crisis" defined in this way belongs to ruling-class ideology because it legitimates demands by capital and state for the top-down reorganization of the economy, political system and state, and social life.

At the level of modern historiography, it has been suggested that

the idea of a standard revolutionary situation in which an economic catastrope raises the desperate and rootless poor against their betters ... has probably disappeared forever ... economic crises are only likely to stimulate rebellion under very special circumstances: when they place the powerful in the position of withholding or extracting resources from organized groups of persons who have established claims on these resources.[32]

At the level of social theory, critical theorists have argued convincingly that human labor or material production is only one (albeit the most important) mediation between human beings and their environment, hence that the methodological

---

[31] Alain Touraine, "Crisis or transformation?", in Norman Birnbaum (ed.), *Beyond the Crisis* (New York, 1977); James O'Connor, "The democratic movement in the United States," *Kapitalistate*, 7 (1978). See also Russell Jacoby, "Narcissism and the crisis of capitalism," *Telos*, 44 (Summer 1980); Robert Alford, *Health Care Politics: Ideological and Interest Group Barriers to Reform* (Chicago, 1975), xi–xii.

[32] Lynn Lees and Charles Tilly, "The people of June, 1848," Center for Research on Social Organization, Working Paper no. 70, University of Michigan (February 1972), 4.

premises of traditional Leninism are unsound, excepting insofar as the party defines *itself* as the social and political mediation. Today it is a commonplace in neo-Marxist thought that human consciousness itself has a constitutive role in the construction of social reality, and that human emancipation cannot be based solely or mainly on "objective" economic conditions and roles, or merely bad fits between economic conditions and capitalist ideology. The word "crisis" is soaked with social, political, and cultural meanings, and the connections between economic crisis, consciousness, and social action are mediated by these social concepts at many different levels of human experience. In particular, the fusion of economic, social-political, and ideological concepts of crisis in the mass media means that a kind of permanent crisis consciousness exists independently of classical capitalist economic "laws of motion."

Perhaps most important, the actual historical development of "late" capitalist societies since World War II has thrown into doubt traditional meanings of "economic crisis," which can no longer be regarded as an "autonomous" process. First, critical theorists and Italian neo-Marxists have demonstrated that society and culture are deeply implicated in the process of capital accumulation. The result is the "social factory," which has given birth to "new social movements" based on struggles around processes of social reproduction in general and the "centrality of the body" in particular. These new social movements cannot be understood in terms of traditional Marxist economic and social theory but rather demand new kinds of economic sociology. In theories of the social factory and new social movements, social struggle is no longer explicable in terms of "the logic of capitalist development or dysfunctions in the system's integrative mechanisms," but rather "the existence of structural antagonism must be socially established," since "the production characteristic of advanced societies requires that control reach beyond the productive structure into the areas of consumption, services, and social relations."[33] Alberto Melucci continues:

[33] Alberto Melucci, "The new social movements: a theoretical approach," *Social Science Information*, 19, 2 (1980), 209, 217. A recent example of the

the struggle centers around the issue of group identity; there is a return to the criterion of ascriptive membership (sex, race, age, locality) which is the form taken by revolt against change directed from above. The movements also have instrumental objectives and seek advantages within the political system, but this dimension is secondary in comparison to the search for solidarity and in comparison to the expressive nature of the relations found in them.[34]

Second, neo-Marxism stresses that politics and state policy are deeply enmeshed in modern capitalist accumulation.[35] The deep interpenetration between state and capital, politics and the market, means that modern "political capitalism" is inexplicable in terms of conventional economic and political theory. Instead, it is argued that we need new kinds of political economic theories which explain economic crisis in relation to political processes and dynamics. These have included the theory of the fiscal crisis of the state, according to which economic crisis tendencies are displaced into (or find their expression in) the state finances of modern capitalism.[36] They have also included the theory that the historical limits of modern capitalism can no longer be plausibly defined in terms of the economic contradictions of modern capitalism but must now be defined in terms of the limitations of the political and

---

growing literature on struggles over collective consumption and local power (i.e. control of social reproduction) is Manuel Castells, *The City and the Grassroots: a Cross-Cultural Theory of Urban Social Movements* (Berkeley, Cal., 1983).

[34] Melucci, "The new social movements," 220. See also Joel Kovel, "Narcissism and the family," *Telos*, 44 (Summer 1980), 99.

[35] The standard work is Andrew Shonfield, *Modern Capitalism: The Changing Balance of Public and Private Power* (New York, 1965). One of the best studies of state economic planning is Stephen S. Cohen, *Modern Capitalist Planning: The French Model* (New York, 1969).

[36] James O'Connor, *The Fiscal Crisis of the State* (New York, 1973). See also Ian Gough, *The Political Economy of the Welfare State* (London, 1978); "Banks: skating on thin ice," *Monthly Review* (February 1975), as well as many other *Monthly Review* "reviews of the month"; David Gold, "The rise and decline of the Keynesian coalition," *Kapitalistate*, 6 (Fall 1977); Clarence Lo, "The conflicting functions of US military spending after World War II," *Kapitalistate*, 3 (Spring 1975). In the 1980s, countless books and articles have appeared which have identified different "problems" of the Keynesian epoch.

state equilibrating mechanisms and legitimation capacities designed to manage these contradictions.[37] In Habermas's words, "if governmental crisis management fails, it lags behind the programmatic demands that it has placed on itself. The penalty for this failure is withdrawal of legitimation."[38] More specifically, Claus Offe advances the theory of

system crises of capitalist societies . . . which seeks out crisis-prone developments not *in the exchange sphere itself* – i.e. on the basis of an *economic* crisis theory – but rather *in the relationship between the three fundamental organizational principles* of society as a whole [the family-normative, business-calculative, and state-coercive]. Not the self-negation of the exchange principle, but rather the question of whether it has been overlaid and challenged by the two alternative organizational principles would be the criterion of crisis processes.

In particular, crisis-proneness is explained by "the development of the normative and political subsystems . . . which infringe on the dominance of the sphere regulated by the exchange of equivalents, namely, the economy." Offe continues: "the more the capitalist economy is forced to utilize 'external regulatory services,' the more precarious becomes its problem of prevailing against the inner dynamics of these 'extraterritorial' systems and of safeguarding itself against encroachments by them." The problem thus arises – one which Offe implies has no permanent answer – of "*politically regulating the economic system without materially politicizing it*, i.e. negating it."[39] This becomes a greater problem, the more that popular participation democra-

---

[37] Claus Offe, "'Crisis of crisis management': elements of a political crisis theory," *International Journal of Politics*, 6 (1977).

[38] Jürgen Habermas, *Legitimation Crisis* (Boston, Mass., 1975), 69. As mentioned above, there are those who believe that "successful accumulation is not contradictory to the achievement of legitimation, but rather one of its preconditions" (Zimmermann, "The study of crises in liberal democracies," 321–22).

[39] Offe, "'Crisis of crisis management': elements of a political crisis theory," 34–5, 51–2.

tizes state administration and the decommodification of life weakens the normative power of possessive individualism.[40]

Other lines of neo-Marxist reasoning have focused on the state's incapacity to develop coherent policies for capital as a whole, owing to the pluralistic structure of the state and/or the competing interests of individual capitals.[41] Because political parties, parliaments, and the separate state agencies are incapable of solving problems arising from malfunctions of the system as a whole, more and different kinds of issues have to be dealt with at the uppermost levels of the state executive. This is thought to pose serious problems of administrative rationality (as well as of political legitimacy).[42] Finally, a number of writers have analyzed the specifically political contradictions of modern political capitalism. Alan Wolfe has comprehensively summarized the many-sided problem of the "limits of legitimacy."[43] Wolfe and others have developed theories of modern political parties which attempt to explain the inability of capitalist governments and states to follow accumulation

[40] However, as Jean Cohen writes, Offe "refrains from deducing the conflict potential of social actors" because of their new and complex identities: Jean L. Cohen, "Between crisis management and social movements: the place of institutional reform," *Telos*, 52 (Summer 1982), 23.

[41] Offe writes that "the common interests of the ruling class are most accurately expressed in those legislative and administrative strategies of the state apparatus which are not initiated by articulated interests, that is, 'from outside,' but which arise from the state organizations' own routines and formal structures": "Structural problems of the capitalist state," in Klaus von Beyme (ed.), *German Political Studies*, I 1975. Offe shows that there exists a selection or filter system within the state, biased in the direction of capitalist interests, which informs decision-making and policy, and which functions at the level of state structure, process, repression, and ideology. According to Offe, however, Marxist neo-orthodoxy has the burden of proof to show that these selection mechanisms actually work in favor of capital as a whole.

[42] Claus Offe, "Notes on the 'laws of motion' of reformist state policies," MS. Offe has shown that in the field of technical education, for example, social democratic politicy oriented to the systemic needs of capital as a whole tends to be subverted or sabotaged by individual capitals and capitalist fractions.

[43] Alan Wolfe, *The Limits of Legitimacy: Political Contradictions of Contemporary Capitalism* (New York, 1977).

policies in systematic ways in the pre-Reagan epoch.[44] Particularly when political parties which were once instruments of the working class or labor unions become parties of national government, social democratic and laborist political leaders tend to lose their grip on the masses; the political system is less able to channel and resolve conflict;[45] the unions tend to replace longstanding ties with socialist, social democratic, and communist parties and seek neo-corporatist solutions to the problems facing labor and the working class.

More specifically, Offe has argued that to the degree that social democratic and labor parties in fact support policies favoring capitalist accumulation, the contradiction between capitalism as such and democratic social and economic policy is displaced into the internal structures of the parties themselves. Horizontal cleavages which divide members and functionaries tend to develop within labor and social democratic parties, hence shifting conflict into non-traditional channels; vertical cleavages which divide "factions" tend to develop in conservative parties.[46] These and other studies by Offe, Habermas, Wolfe, and other neo- and post-Marxist theorists in effect explain why the choice has not yet been made between "socialism and barbarism," and why the consequences of modern social democracy (including its variants such as laborism, New Dealism, spoils allotment systems, and democratic corporatism) are necessarily economically and politically ambiguous. These studies also indicate some of the reasons why the class struggle has been so fractionalized, displaced, and difficult to organize politically. In sum, neo-Marxist writers

[44] Alan Wolfe, "Political parties and capitalist development," *Kapitalistate*, 6 (Fall 1977).

[45] Claus Offe, "The separation of form and content in liberal democracy," in Claus Offe, *Contradictions of the Welfare State* (Cambridge, Mass., 1984), 166.

Offe argues that, from the standpoint of conflicting interests in civil society, democratic politics in principle functions as an arena of struggle; from the standpoint of the state, the democratic political process is supposed to resolve conflict. Democratic politics thus "allows for articulation and resolution of conflict . . . by organizing "diversity and unity."

[46] Claus Offe, letter to the author.

have in one way or another stressed that the parliament and state are part and parcel of the economic structures and processes of modern capitalism – that is a kind of material, ideological, and institutional embodiment of capitalist competition and accumulation. Increasingly, not only the elected branch but also the state apparatus itself is seen as an arena of struggle to impose (and resist) capitalist forms of activity within state agencies and between these agencies and private capital and material life generally.[47]

There is a third and final historical development of "late" capitalist society which has thrown doubt on traditional meanings of "economic crisis." Critical theorists and neo-Marxists emphasize that society and culture, including family and gender relations, have come to be increasingly politically administered by the state. It is argued that modern "administered society" renders conventional political and social analysis more or less irrelevant and instead requires new kinds of political sociology and a critical social psychology. Alain Touraine, for example, argues that the technological expansion of capital and the centralization of state power require more social control of social reproduction. The opposing forces of technocracy and community control "overload ... mechanisms of political negotiation." Hence modern social conflict arises between the "apparatus" (technocracy) and the "territory" (community) over dominant social definitions of identity, morality, and social norms.[48] The idea of administered society, with somewhat different conclusions, has also been used by Joachim Hirsch. He maintains that the coexistence (in German) of bourgeois parliamentary and constitutional institutions alongside constitutional violations and the growing use of state repression may be

---

[47] Nicos Poulantzas, *State, Power, Socialism* (London, 1978); O'Connor, "The democratic movement in the United States;" Gosta Epsing-Anderson, Roger Friedland, and Erik Olin Wright, "Modes of class struggle and the capitalist state," *Kapitalistate*, 4–5 (1976); Francis Fox Piven and Richard A. Cloward, *The New Class War* (New York, 1982) ("A century and a half after the achievement of formal democratic rights, the state has finally become the main arena of class conflict" (124)).

[48] Touraine, "Crisis or transformation?", 35.

explained in terms of the contradictory unity of bourgeois political rule based on ideological integration and forceful repression in an epoch in which "the state has penetrated into spheres of life previously considered 'private.'"[49]

In a different approach to the dynamics of "administered society," Jürgen Habermas has described modern capitalism as "social welfare mass democracy." According to him,

the rationalization of social life, or the extension of subsystems of purposive-rational action beyond the confines of the market, law, and the administration, generates a dynamic whose consequences may undermine the very legitimacy of such rationalization processes ... the extension of administrative-instrumental contol may lead to its own process of demystification. Domination does not become anonymous. As the process of its own generation becomes transparent through the apparent intervention of the political apparatus into all domains of social life, domination relations may be subjected to increased legitimation demands.[50]

[49] Joachim Hirsch, "The crisis of mass integration: on the development of political repression in Federal Germany," *International Journal of Urban and Regional Research*, 3 (1978). "The state has penetrated into spheres of life previously considered 'private,' has extended its regulatory functions into areas that were hitherto unregulated, has alternatively repressed and 'normalized' the organization of labor, consumption, and reproduction, and has marginalized and controlled would-be 'deviant' populations. This qualitatively new form of state-administered crisis and conflict management has generated new terrains of conflict within and against the state. Hirsch has described this process of statification as the 'security state,' denoting precisely the fusion of welfare functions with a technically perfected 'surveillance state'": Margit Mayer, "Through the eye of the needle," MS (August 1981).

On the other hand, according to Offe, crises of administrative rationality have forced the state to "contract out" more state functions to private agencies. This creates a corporatist-type model in which representatives of interest groups constantly bargain for position and advantages. Power thus becomes decentralized and structures which constrain state policy in the interest of capital are weakened: Claus Offe, "Notes on the future of European socialism and the state," *Kapitalistate*, 7 (1978).

[50] Seyla Benhabib, "Modernity and the aporias of critical theory," *Telos*, 49 (Fall 1981), 50, summing up a central line of analysis in Habermas, *Legitimation Crisis*. Benhabib continues: "The crux of Habermas' argument is the analysis of those mechanisms through which economic and administrative rationality crises can lead to a legitimation and motivation crisis. In late capitalist societies, such crises can occur only when, under the conditions of

In sum, in the study of modern capitalism, it is no longer useful to view economic, social, and political life as if they were separate spheres of organization and activity. The "new and close articulation between the economy, the state, and ideology" (in Poulantzas's words), or the interpenetration between norms of economic efficiency and legal-rational political and moral-normative social norms in effect abolishes autonomous "economic laws" defined in neo-orthodox Marxist terms. Capitalism rather becomes "mixed" in the sense of combining in seemingly fateless and ambiguous ways diverse features of capital logic, social life and social struggles, politics, and state forms and contents. When economy, society, and state cannot be conceived except as relations of class and social struggles, the interpenetration of individual and citizen roles in political capitalism, consumer and worker roles in the social factory, and citizen and consumer roles in the administered society – all mediating and being mediated by both the law of value and one another – the crucial task of modern crisis theory is to develop a unified "field theory" based on the interpenetration of economic, social, and political crisis tendencies in ways which have not been systematically studied within the framework of modern historical materialism.

A beginning has been made in the form of the "class struggle" theory of crisis, which attempts to link modern crisis with social and political movements of oppressed minorities in the imperialist countries, social movements of "marginal populations," national liberation movements, women's struggles, and so on. In a similar vein, Manuel Castells argues that modern economic crisis is "caused by a general process of social

---

the repoliticization of the relations of production, the depoliticization of the population and their manipulation to accept technocratic, nonparticipatory ideologies can no longer be secured. But – and this is Habermas' ground for rejecting the thesis of the reification of domination – *the manipulative production of legitimation becomes destructive as soon as the mode of its production becomes visible*: 'there is no administrative generation of meaning. . . . A crisis of legitimation can be expected when expectations are generated that cannot be satisfied within available patterns of value and through other compensatory mechanisms. Legitimation crises must be based on a motivational crisis" (ibid., 51).

disruption in the most advanced capitalist societies."[51] Social disorganization has "called into question the structure of social relationships underlying the pattern of capital accumulation . . . and triggered the structural tendencies toward a falling rate of profit." These lines of theoretical attack are a vast improvement over Marxist neo- orthodoxy because they link social structure and social organization with economic crisis and the determinants of the profit rate.

Habermas is perhaps the best-known exponent of the view that "the laws of the economic system are no longer identical to those analyzed by Marx" because of "interference from the political system," hence creating the need for a new theory of the "interaction of economics, politics, and culture."[52] Habermas advances a crisis theory which tries to combine "objective" and "subjective" methods, without falling into either determinist or voluntarist thinking. He writes: "to conceive of a process as a crisis is tacitly to give it normative meaning – the resolution of the crisis affects a liberation of the subject caught up in it." In traditional Marxist terms, "subject" has the twofold meaning of "capital," which is understood as the systematic and historically specific process of valorization, and "working class," which is construed as self-conscious, organized, and combative

---

[51] Manuel Castells, *The Economic Crisis and American Society* (Princeton, NJ, 1980), 5; "we do not see the theory of class struggle and the theory of the falling rate of profit as contradictory but as complementary. This is because the first explains the effects of society on capital and the second the effects of capital on society" (ibid., 25). A summary of the history of the idea that "capital" means "class struggle" can be found in Harry Cleaver's *Reading Capital Politically* (Austin, Texas, 1979), "Introduction."

[52] Angelo Bolaffi, "An interview with Jürgen Habermas," *Telos*, 39 (Spring 1979), 168. It should be mentioned that Habermas fails to deal with the problem of "interference from the political system" in Marx's time, nor does he consider the ways in which Marx and Engels treated this issue theoretically and historically.

In another interview, Habermas poses the problem thus: "Because Hegelian-Marxist social theory, developed in categories of totality, has decomposed into its parts, namely, action theory and systems theory, the present task now consists of combining these two paradigms in a non-trivial fashion": Alex Honneth et al., "The dialectics of rationalization: an interview with Jürgen Habermas," *Telos*, 49 (Fall 1981), 13.

human subjectivity during economic crises. "Liberation" in the first sense means successful crisis-induced capital restructuring, or the restoration of the conditions of capitalist accumulation. In the second sense "liberation" means social and political transformation (and, at the limit, revolution), i.e. freedom from the pain and suffering which economic crises magnify.[53] In neo-Marxism, however, "liberation" assumes the additional meaning of freedom from crisis-induced powerlessness, threats to the individual's social identity, and the loss of what it is possible to accept in matter-of-fact ways. These latter meanings of crisis as an "ordeal" underwrite neo-Marxist concepts of emancipation, because liberation from the pain and suffering of crisis-induced unemployment, economic insecurity, and poverty alone can be affected (however imperfectly and temporarily) by the restoration of capital's "normal sovereignty," i.e. renewal of profitable conditions of capitalist accumulation.

Habermas tries to demonstrate that liberation defined in terms of social identity, social practice, and power cannot be fruitfully discussed within the framework of the neo-orthodox Marxist theory of accumulation, which he defines as a variety of "systems theory" (however dialectical its method; hence, however large the gulf between Marxist orthodoxy and bourgeois systems theory). Without really coming to terms with Marx's theory of class struggle and revolution on its own grounds, his argument is that "action theory" is also needed. Echoing the critique of Leninism presented earlier, Habermas writes that

systems are not presented as subjects, but only subjects can be involved in crises ... only when members of society experience structural alterations as critical for continued existence and feel their social identity threatened can we speak of crises. *Disturbances of system integration endanger continued existence only to the extent that social integration is at stake*, that is, only when the consensual foundations of normative structures are so much impaired that society

---

[53] Richard Sennett, "Destructive Gemeinschaft," in Norman Birnbaum (ed.), *Beyond the Crisis* (New York, 1977), 171.

becomes anomic. Crisis states assume the form of a disintegration of social institutions.[54]

Habermas's formulation of the problem suggests that his method may be a kind of radical Durkheimianism. His distinction between economic-system integration and social integration suggests possibilities for radical improvements of traditional Marxist objectivism, on the one hand, and voluntarism, on the other. In Durkheimian thought, system integration requires that system functions are integrated into one another. Social integration requires that individuals are normatively integrated into particular system functions, and thus fulfill expected economic and social roles. The difference between system and social integration suggests a taxonomy of crisis possibilities which Habermas himself does not develop, but which is implicit (in a different form) in "class struggle" crisis theory.

Methodologically, economic-system crisis depends on the assumption that labor power is the *object* of exchange alone, hence that the wage bargain obeys the "laws of motion" of capitalist accumulation. It also assumes that the worker is the *object* of labor alone, i.e. that the worker's labor power is "consumed" by capital, that the worker has no control of the labor process. Finally, system crisis theory presupposes that the product of labor is a commodity, strictly defined, i.e. that all needs are satisfied in the commodity form. It is obvious from this brief account that system crisis theory by definition rules out class struggle in the money, productive, and commodity circuits of capital, respectively.

By contrast, "class struggle" crisis theory is a species of social crisis theory. It depends on the assumption that labor power is

---

[54] Habermas, *Legitimation Crisis*, 3 (my italics). This is echoed by John Keane, who writes that "the truth of the old crisis theorem remains, the renewal of subjectivity continues to depend on the decay of this system's objective structure and signification" ("Crisis in the industrial world?", 188). This is also the theme of Daniel Bell's work, which stresses the absence of any deep-rooted morality of belief system, which is thought to threaten capitalism's survival most profoundly: *The Cultural Contradiction of Capitalism* (New York, 1979), *passim*.

not only the object but also the subject of exchange, that is, that wages depend on collective action as well as on the "laws of motion" of capitalism. It also presupposes that the worker is the subject as well as object of labor, that the labor process depends on collective action and is inscribed by autonomous worker struggles as well as the "valorization" of capital. Last, "class struggle" crisis theory assumes that the product of labor is not a pure commodity, hence that needs to one degree or another are satisfied directly in the social form rather than in reified ways through the mediation of commodities.

Neo-orthodox Marxist theories of economic crisis, defined as systemic ruptures in the circuits of capital, exemplify system crisis theory, or system disintegration. Class struggle is assumed to have little or nothing to do with deficiencies of money capital to advance for constant and variable capital, the absence of sufficient labor power or means and objects of production within the immediate process of production, and/or shortages of revenues to realize total values produced. As we saw in chapter 2, in neo-orthodox Marxism, liquidity crises, crises of supply of productive inputs, and realization crises are systemically produced by movements of the value composition of capital, rate of exploitation, cost of the elements of capital, international economic relations, and so on.

By contrast, theories of economic crisis defined as ruptures in the circuits of capital which are intentionally or unintentionally produced by direct working-class action exemplify social crisis theory, or social disintegration. Economic-system forces may or may not be assumed to be related to wage struggles which create liquidity crises, struggles against waged work which produce productivity crises; and/or struggles against prices in the sphere of circulation.[55]

---

[55] Cleaver and Bell have worked out "Marxologically' an excellent and more comprehensive taxonomy similar to the one offered above. But, like Marx himself, they do not distinguish between system and social crisis, class-imposed functional integration from class-imposed social integration. Hence, they do not articulate the relationship between the "system" and the "social" in politically powerful ways: "Marx's crisis theory as a theory of class relations," *Research in Political Economy*, 5 (1982).

The important point in this connection is that social disintegration may or may not result in system disintegration. Social struggles which disrupt the circuits of capital may or may not be functional for capitalist-system integration. If we imagine wage struggles interrupting the money circuit; sabotage, struggles against technological change, or environmental struggles interrupting the productive circuit; self-reduction in prices, mass theft, or consumer boycotts interrupting the commodity circuit – all traveling through the circuits of capital (which thus function as vehicles or avenues of worker struggle) – there occurs a combination of system and social disintegrative processes which may or may not reinforce one another. Worker struggles may be system-stabilizing or system-destabilizing. Wage struggles may resolve systemic problems of value realization; stoppages in production which reduce the amount of money capital advanced for labor power may help resolve liquidity problems; self-reduction of prices may help resolve credit crises and/or destabilizing inflation. Whether or not these results occur does not depend on the logical conditions of the system- and social-theory models but on concrete historical conjunctures. For example, it has been argued that worker struggles in the USA until the mid-twentieth century functioned as engines of class recomposition and capital accumulation.[56] Social struggle and social crisis may not create but help to resolve economic-system crisis, when the result of worker struggles bears little or no relationship to intentions, or when there exist historical structural gaps between "objective conditions" and "subjective wills."

It is clear that these approaches to crisis theory (and to the contemporary crisis of capitalism) pertain to the *conditions* of crisis, not crisis *historically understood*. On the one hand, "capital logic" delineates systemic conditions of disruptions or breakages in the money, productive, and commodity circuits of capital. On the other hand, "class struggle logic" delineates social conditions of disjunctures in the circuits of capital. Just as there is a world of difference between the theory of the

[56] O'Connor, *Accumulation Crisis*, chapter 2.

conditions of capitalist accumulation and capitalist development historically understood, there is also a difference between a theory of the conditions of class struggle and crisis, and class struggle and crisis historically understood. Both "capital logic" and "class struggle logic" delineate logical possibilities of crisis, but tend to neglect historical and institutional analysis,[57] as well as the actual social and ideological forms of modern class struggle and crisis. These approaches are effective ways to organize thoughts and empirical data, but they have no direct political relevance because they are not grounded in the concrete analysis of ideologies, institutions, and the historical conjuncture. Both "capital logic" and "class struggle logic" pertain to abstract stresses and strains, tensions, and disjunctures within the process of capitalist accumulation rather than to concrete ideological, institutional, and other contradictions which social classes, class fractions, political parties, and the state seek to mobilize or suppress, ignore or exploit. "Capital logic" and "class struggle logic" are combined in complex and varied ways in real history alone. When these two logics are separated they are useful only for problems of theoretical analysis. When they are combined and historical grounded, theoretical synthesis, hence social and political praxis, become possible.

Even when we enlarge the model to include not only shortages of money capital, labor power, means and objects of production, labor discipline, and effective demand but also financial resources, political and administrative resources, and social motivations and incentives, only logical possibilities present themselves. For example, fiscal deficits may or may not activate motivations and hence legitimation deficits. Reduced

---

[57] In Cohen's view, "system and action theory must remain antinomic if the institutional dimension . . . is not included as an analytic component of social theory. . . . Institutional analysis . . . can be seen as a third analytic level, equally indispensable for critical theory as are systems or action theory. The logic of institutional continuity and discontinuity of modernity is not reducible to either the variation of functions, abstract capacities, or conflictural social action. A society is not only integrated and contested, it is also institutionalized" (Cohen, "Between crisis management and social movements: the place of institutional reform," 35–6).

capacities for administrative rationality or economic steering may or may not reinforce fiscal and/or profits shortages. In the same way that ruptures in the circuits of capital may be conceived as systemically or socially produced, state administrative and fiscal capacity, motivations, and political legitimacy may be conceived in terms of "capital logic" (e.g. neo-Weberianism) or within the framework of social struggles and emancipatory practices (e.g. much if not most of the literature on new social movements). However, the differences between such practices within the circuits of capital, on the one hand, and within society and the state, on the other, are great. Struggles over wages, hours, working conditions, and prices necessarily combine with the capitalist logic of *valorization*. By contrast, in the process of social and political struggle, substantive rationality combines with technical rationality; practical-critical reason with instrumental reason; legitimation defined within working-class organizations and social movements with capitalist state legitimation; social motivations with individual motivations; individuals as historical, social beings with ideologies of individualism and their social practices. Ambiguities and contradictions (which cannot avoid having mild or devastating effects on personality structures) abound in "late" capitalist society.

Social Crisis as Social Struggle

The logicalistic formulations of crisis theory which a reading of both Habermas and "class struggle" theory inspires lead to political dead ends because they do not break sharply enough with neo-orthodox Marxism. In fact, the structural-functionalist premises of Habermas's approach unexpectedly reinforce neo-orthodoxy's theory of "capital logic." The general reason is that the whole problem of social-class composition and recomposition through economic crisis is more or less ignored. It should be obvious that the process of political reproduction – including the reproduction of conditions of political legitimation and administrative rationality – must be fundamentally different when the propertyless working class reaches its majority and wins a wide range of bourgeois democratic rights.[58] In short, political reproduction conditions and political crisis tendencies are inexplicable except in the contexts not only of the accumulation process and economic crisis but also of processes of working-class formation and social recomposition.[59] The specific reason is that neo-Marxism in general (and Habermas in particular) exclude possibilities for emancipation within the productive working class because the capitalist labor process is interpreted as a productive force, or as an instrumental rather than simultaneously a practical-critical social relationship of production. Subjectivity is "squeezed out" of the labor process by tyrannizing science and technology, or modern technological rationalizations of work. Emancipatory potentials are therefore considered to exist only in spheres of activity not yet totally penetrated by capital.[60] These are typically regarded as the main spheres of social reproduction – the state, family, education systems, and so on – in which contradictions within capitalist accumulation in general and the production process in particular are displaced (hence the growth of new social movements of public workers and clients, students, women, minorities, etc.). With the exception that Harry Cleaver includes the active, as well as the latent, reserve army of labor as the source of social and political emancipation, Habermas's approach and "class struggle" theory are surprisingly similar. "As constant capital, especially fixed capital in the form of machines, plays an ever more dominant role in production," Cleaver writes,

[58] As has often been pointed out, delegitimation must be subjectively shared by large numbers of people, who must also be organized and mobilized, for there to occur deep political reform or revolution.

[59] Just as it is ironic that neo-orthodox Marxist economics has no class analysis of the conditions of reproduction of labor power, so it is that neo-Marxist political sociology has no historical sociology of social class and class formation. Both schools of thought appear to be stalled in the same methodological traffic jam.

[60] Bolaffi, "An interview with Jürgen Habermas," 171. Offe seems to agree with this view: "Further comments on Mueller and Neusthuss," *Telos*, 25 (1975), 109.

it becomes more and more difficult for capital to impose commodity producing work as the central social activity. The more difficult it is to impose commodity producing work, the more difficult it is to shape the rest of life around the reproduction of labor-power. As this occurs, *labor as a source of value to capital falls into crisis*. Business must either find new avenues of imposing work, new fields of labor-intensive production, or the mechanisms of its rule will continue to decline, opening wider and wider spaces for working class struggle.'[61]

In Habermas's more theoretically sophisticated, but less materialistically grounded view, "symmetrical and more expressive forms of interaction" are possible only within newly proletarianized sectors, youth cultures, marginal workers, oppressed minorities, and the women's movement. While Habermas brings a general historical dimension to his theory of social crisis and his analysis of "life-world and system,"[62] according to Jean Cohen,

---

[61] Harry Cleaver, "Theses on the Marxian labor theory of value," paper submitted to the special issue of the *Review of Radical Political Economics* (*RRPE*) on "Controversies in the theory of value", July 1, 1981, 14. Cleaver's views are rooted in Marx's theory of accumulation, capital concentration and centralization, growth of an active reserve army, etc. However, it is clear that both Habermas and Cleaver are strongly influenced by the big facts of the late twentieth century, i.e. Third World revolution, black revolts, etc., originating in either the latent and/or active reserve armies of labor.

In an informal conversation, Steven Hymer advanced the outlines of a theory of revolution which roughly resembles the approaches sketched above. The revolution in capitalist production *relations* (Steve said) begins in the latent reserve army, travels through the active reserve army, and ends with the productive workforce. The revolution in the capitalist *forces* of production moves in exactly the opposite direction. (See, for example, James O'Connor, *The Origins of Socialism in Cuba* (Ithaca, NY, 1970).)

[62] "These areas of cultural tradition – social integration through values and norms, education, socialization of coming generations – are . . . ontologically speaking, held together by their very nature through the medium of communicative behavior. Once the steering media such as money and power penetrate these areas, for instance by redefining relations in terms of consumption or by bureaucratizing the conditions of life, then it is more than an attack on traditions. The foundations of a life-world that is already rationalized are under assault. What is at stake is the symbolic reproduction of the life-world itself. In sum, crises that arise in the area of material reproduction are intercepted at the cost of a pathologizing of the life-world" (Honneth et al., "The dialectics of rationalization: an interview with Jürgen Habermas," 22).

what is of interest to [him] is the logic of justification of the interpretations of values and norms within these movements, and not their substantive content of concerns. . . . [For this reason] the reconstruction of the logic of moral-cultural development cannot enter into or explain the *dynamics* of social movements in and through which the battles over interpretation of norms and the creation of new ones are fought. . . . Habermas' theoretical strategy *can* explain the likelihood of crises of social identity and assess the abstract cultural possibilities available for alternative identity construction. But despite the attempt to introduce an action framework into crisis theory, despite the importance of providing a standard with which to assess the character of social movements – they play no constitutive role regarding legitimation, the functioning of the public sphere, or the creation of norms."[63]

A quite different criticism is that Habermas fails to grasp that capital accumulation and class struggle are lived contradictions, or that productive economic (not only social and political) activity is both symmetrical and asymmetrical, expressive and nonexpressive. His formulation loses sight of the fact that real-life communication in the labor process, as well as in the "public sphere" and society generally, exemplifies neither the domination of capital over labor, nor emancipation and free-dom, but rather both simultaneously – albeit in terms of hegemonic ideologies. Real communication and social interac-tion in class society, which is also divided by ideologies and practices of racism, sexism, national chauvinism, and individualism, are characterized by ambiguities of thought,

---

"Until now the processes of destruction that have paved the way to capitalist modernization have occurred in such a way as to give rise to new institutions. These new institutions transferred social material from the realm of sovereignty of the life-world into realms of action steered by the media and organized by formal law. This went well as long as it only touched on functions of material reproduction that need not unconditionally be organized communicatively. In the meantime, however, it seems that the system's imperatives are attacking areas of action which are demonstrably unable to perform their own tasks if they are removed from communicatively structured areas of action. This involves tasks such as cultural reproduction, social integration and socialization" (ibid., 18).

[63] Cohen, "Between crisis management and social movements," 28–9.

feelings, and action which are the result of, and also socially constructed into, "contradictions" – hence the importance of social-theoretical decoding methods for the critique of the capitalist labor process, crisis theory, and political practice.[64]

Hence also the fact that social institutions do not simply "disintegrate," but instead are subverted or destroyed by new "proto-institutions," however informal, temporary, or invisible to the media and social science. "Destruction and deformation are interlaced with new growth and new formations."[65] In this alternative view of labor, culture, and crisis, society does not become simply "disrupted" or "anomic" or "normless," but rather is torn by competing and contradictory norms which develop within and between social groups. Social integration as

[64] In the USA, David Montgomery has demonstrated the coexistence of practical-critical reason with instrumental rationality within the capitalist labor process (although it must be added that his demonstration is more convincing when he discusses the late nineteenth-century skilled worker): *Workers' Control in America* (New York, 1979.)

For a conceptual redefinition of productive labor which attempts to grasp the deep ambiguities in the capitalist labor process and the coexistence of capital and class struggle, see James O'Connor, "Productive and unproductive labor," *Politics and Society*, 5 (1975). The key point to be made in connection with this question is that practical-critical activity of the working class within the labor process occurs within ideological forms, especially (in the USA) ideologies and practices of individualism.

[65] Honneth et al., "The dialectics of rationalization: an interview with Jürgen Habermas," 27.

John Keane writes that "Kuhn's recent historiographical appropriation of the concept of 'crisis' rightly stresses its signification of a process of destruction *and* construction, of unsettling anomaly *and* intervention against the old normality. . . . With reference to crisis-ridden social processes, this means that the disintegration of the 'natural attitudes' of those who have become objects of system paralysis facilitates both an expanded awareness of this objective paralysis and active attempts to overcome it": John Keane, "Bureaucracy and its discontents: crisis tendencies of the welfare state," MS, London, August 1981, 3.

In the same vein, Jean Cohen adds that Habermas's argument that "legitimation deficits would lead to crises if accompanied by motivation deficits implies a standpoint that *abstractly opposes social integration to social disintegration*. . . . social movements are perforce relegated to a residual category of social action that is either anomic or reactionary . . . social movements are viewed as crisis phenomena *tout court*" ("Between crisis management and social movements," 29, my italics).

such is not at stake, but rather what *kind* of social integration regulated by what *kinds* of norms, goals, and practices. A historical-materialist concept of crisis needs, therefore, to restore the dialectical unity between "objectivity" and "subjectivity," or between "theory" and "practice," which permits us to grasp "crisis" as the development of new social and political practices which threaten existing social institutions and/or structures.[66]

In this sense, crisis defined as "turning point" exists when new power centers confront existing structures of domination, when individual identity is split between contradictory premises, when it is generally unknown what can be taken for granted or expected from existing or emerging roles, institutions, and social practices. "Crisis" defined in this way has weak status in neo-orthodox Marxist thought (albeit stronger status in neo-Marxism), and no status whatsoever in bourgeois thought, because within its undialectical problematic new social relationships are understood as building on, gradually replacing, or adapting to older relationships and practices – that is, boundary lines between older and emerging social processes, values, and norms are blurred by processes of mutual adaptation or mystified by only apparent resemblances between old and new.

---

[66] "In all of Marx's work capitalist crisis is, from the point of view of the working-class subject, a moment not of *breakdown* but of break*through*. If crises for capital are basically its loss of control (direct or indirect) over the working class, then we can turn this relation around and see that they are simultaneously the eruption of working-class subjectivity that undermines capitalist control" (Cleaver and Bell, "Marx's crisis theory as a theory of class relations," 258).

"Crisis and class struggle are articulated so profoundly that the first takes on, within this antagonistic dialectic, the form of catastrophe and the second takes on the form of communism – the real, physical pole of an implacable will necessary to eliminate the adversary . . . the catastrophies for capital are the party, the deployment of communist subjectivity, and revolutionary will and organization" (Negri, *Marx Beyond Marx*, 9).

The Hegelian-Marxist ambience of "class struggle" crisis theory, which is based on the "identity principle" in philosophy, and which sociologically does not separate functions from people, is nowhere better exemplified than in these powerful lines, which have led to political dead ends.

A social-scientific view adequate to the task of comprehending the modern crisis interprets the roots of both decadent or blocked social processes and emancipatory possibilities as immanent in the same human critical practises.[67] Put boldly, crisis is not anomie or social disintegration but social struggle and social reintegration. This definition of social crisis is faithful to historical fact because, when crises – defined as threats to dominant social relationships – "break out," those social classes and class fractions and ascriptive and "quasi-groups" which cling most tenaciously to old ways of thinking and acting (not to speak of material and ideological resources) fight back most violently, in this way creating conditions for historical ruptures and transformations. Social struggles develop in which traditional power centers try to reinforce, defend, or reform old structures of domination and control.[68] The greater the threat from emerging centers of power (everything else being the same), the greater the resistance thrown up by the old. In this sense, the essence of crisis is not social disintegration but social struggle. As Marx, Engels, and Lenin's political writings amply testify, it is only the forms and violence of the resistance of established power which test fully the strength of the emerging opposition. When new social forces strengthen themselves through struggle to overcome the hardening resistance of old centers of power, there occurs a conjuncture in which the dominant social relationships may be reformed or overthrown.

[67] Jean Cohen writes that "social movements are the process through which social identities are constituted, and the institutionalized norms and hierarchical stratification system of a given social order, challenged": "Between crisis management and social movements," 31, referring to Alain Touraine's *The Voice and the Eye* (New York, 1981).

[68] A subtle account of the dialectics of violence and cooptation by the state faced with different kinds of "new social movements" is Margit Mayer, "Urban social movements and beyond: new linkages between movement sectors and the state in West Germany and the United States," paper prepared for delivery at the Fifth International Conference of Europeanists, Washington, DC, October 18–20, 1985. The same author has described the proposed restructuring or transformation (rather than dismantling) of the West German welfare state by the Christian Democratic Party: "The political processing of urban grassroots demands: a comparative exploration of shifts in the pattern of citizen interest intermediation," MS (September 1984).

Or old power centers may succeed in smashing or taming the standard bearers of the new social practices, which may subsequently be adapted to the needs of the dominant social groups and relationships.

In either case, the struggles of old powers to defend themselves by reinforcing their particular structures of domination are themselves costly, not only to the attacking but also to the defending forces. Social struggles which constitute crisis moments in which objective and subjective processes seemingly collapse into a single combat, but which remain structurally distinct in the social and individual "unconscious," invariably raise the material, ideological, and political stakes. Gains and losses become combined historical processes; crisis resolution expresses itself not only as the abatement of struggle but also as the "capitalization" of gains, the rebuilding of weakened structures of domination, the abandonment of previously strategic defensive positions, and the adaptation of old ideologies. Failures of social movements to restructure society lead back to obsessive capitalist accumulation with new layers of ideological legitimations. By contrast, successful struggle is based not only on the practical critique of dominant ideologies and the reconstruction of social relationships, but also on the *self-destruction* of capital and its ideologies suffered in the course of its counter-attack to prevent new social relationships from destroying older ones.

According to this theory of social crisis, accumulation, fiscal, and legitimation crises, crises of authority and administrative rationality, and motivations crises mean that dominant norms and social mechanisms can no longer be accepted in a matter-of-fact way. For example, it cannot be taken for granted that political consensus through established patterns of coalition-building is feasible; that the state can steer the capitalist economy successfully; or that fiscal stability is possible. Men cannot accept matter-of-factly that women will perform their traditional roles without a fight. Cynicism is merely one element in an ensemble of contradictory crisis attitudes and, while "normal" social and individual capacities are in part or whole crippled or lost, human capacities are at the same moment redefined. Political leaders may build new fighting coalitions;

communities may reconstruct steering mechanisms or invent new ones; workers may adopt new attitudes and practices in relation to technology and its uses, the labor process and the product of labor, and the meaning of social reproduction as a whole.[69]

The significance of this line of analysis is not merely that human ideological and practical interventions are needed to resolve crisis through social reintegration, but also (and most importantly) that crises in established institutions and social and economic processes are *produced* through reconstituted human interventions which the contradictions of capital and capitalist society, especially the ideological contradictions, make possible. Contradictions within the productive circuit of capital; problematic will-formation and determination of needs; uncertain personal motivations within the sphere of consumption; irrationalities within the money and commodity circuits of capital; chaos within the spheres of capitalist competition and state administration; and questionable political participation and divided loyalties – all these not only "result" from crisis but also may have more or less powerful independent effects on valorization, the profit rate, the rate and stability of capital accumulation, as well as social order and political legitimation.

Neo-orthodox Marxist and other crisis theories which interpret social movements merely as reactions to crisis symptoms thus can be seen to be fatalistic. By contrast, crisis theory which accepts that social movements battle in fields against and *within* the law of value, against and *within* the state and society, and against and *within* hegemonic ideologies are not fatalistic. It is true that, under well-defined conditions, neo-orthodox Marxism and much if not all of neo-Marxism may be able to "predict the future." However (excluding Lenin's "tactical science"), they can rarely judge "what can be made to happen in the

---

[69] There is plenty of evidence to support the view that the majority of citizens in Western democracies are politically apathetic (defined in mainstream terms), even during economic hard times. On the other hand, local action, community organization and politics, alternative politics, single-issue politics, solidarity movements, etc., seem to flourish today.

future" precisely because they are not immersed in prefigurative and combative social practices. Social-scientific crisis theory must therefore be formulated in terms of what has been made to happen in history and what can be made to happen in the future, rather than in terms of what has happened and what probably will happen. Crisis theory meaningfully explains social action when, and only when, it has become a weapon in the hands of contemporary social and working-class movements which seek "to make the future the present."

This line of reasoning throws some light on why both Marxist orthodoxy and neo-Marxism continue to separate economic theory from social-political theory, and why the "class struggle" school neglects social-political theory. Figuratively speaking, in the neo-orthodox Marxist party, economic crisis theory remains in the hands of specialized economists, while political theory is the monopoly of the central committee. In the politically chaotic world of neo-Marxism, subjectivity is reintroduced at the level of analysis of social and political processes, but economic theory remains separate or is purged from the study of sociology and historical materialism. The possibility that crises are socially constructed rather than systematically created underscores the limitations of the neo-orthodox Marxist medical model of crisis, in which there is no room for human subjects to create their own crises. By contrast, neo-Marxism and post-Marxism at their best stress that crisis is a "process of destruction *and* construction, challenge *and* response, of unsettling anomaly and nascent attempts to proliferate interpretive responses which subvert old normality."[70]

The Working-Class Movement and Contemporary Crisis

A plausible theory of the contemporary crisis of capitalism and imperialism is that it originated in the contingent and contradictory practices of capital, the working-class movement, and new

---

[70] Keane, "Crisis in the industrial world?", 184.

social movements – that is, social struggle, rather than the "systemic economic contradictions of capitalism." In this sense, such a theory belongs to the family of "class struggle" crisis theories. The question immediately arises, what and where are the working-class and new social movements? Open and violent conflict between capital and labor on a large scale occurs only in pre-revolutionary situations and periods of political revolution and counter-revolution (such as Russia in 1917, Cuba in 1959–63, Chile in 1970–3). In non-revolutionary situations, open class and/or social warfare is absent by definition. Is the workers' movement therefore the struggle over wages, hours, and working conditions alone? Or, more broadly, the struggle against productivity within the productive circuit of capital? Or, even more broadly, the struggle against prices, e.g. to control rents, depress interest rates, or fight inflation? Or should the concept of working-class movement be stretched to include struggles *within* the working class to overcome ideological divisions and establish principles of unity which function as the basis for collective will-formation and social praxis?[71] To raise this question suggests the enormity of the theoretical problem of developing a "theory of class struggle" which includes but also contrasts with Marx's critique of political economy, or the "class struggle of theories."

In the USA (to take one example) class and social struggle assume as many forms as there are forms of economic, social, and political life. Social struggles infuse the social factory, political capitalism, and the administered society. The division of social labor is crisis-ridden; changes in the division of labor are crisis-dependent; thus the universality of particularistic regional and national struggles, struggles over ethnic and gender identity, community struggles. Most relevant in the present context, Marx himself stressed that social struggles historically assume ideological forms which may make it appear that class struggle as such does not exist. For example, in Roman slavery, class struggle was partly fought out in terms of the juridical rights of human beings who were also bonded

---

[71] Nicos Poulantzas, *State, Power, Socialism* (London, 1980).

slaves. In feudal Europe, based on religious domination as well as open violence, class struggle assumed the form of religious warfare. In pre-revolutionary France, class conflict was fought in terms of Estate rights and privileges.

In the capitalist mode of production, Marx stressed that the basic contradiction is between social production and individual appropriation of the social product. The traditional Marxist formulation, however, did not emphasize sufficiently the contradiction between social production and individualistic forms of production – that "individualist forms," such as competition between workers on the shop floor, disorganize the working class, not only in production but also in exchange and consumption, not to speak of social reproduction generally, including the reproduction of politics and the state.[72] Ideologies of individualism and ideological practices (especially in the USA) inhere in the wage and commodity forms of material life and in forms of social and political life. Working-class struggle "in-itself" occurs *within* the wage form, commodity form, and individualistic social and political forms. These include trade-unionism, consumerism, environmentalism, and social democracy, which are typically characterized by the use of collective means for individualist ends. In a society of individual property owners, including individual ownership of labor power and means of consumption, worker struggle "in-itself" necessarily takes the forms of individual or collective struggles for individual goals and ends. The reason that neo-Marxism does not normally formulate the issue in this way is doubtless because the abyss between social production, the division of industrial and social labor, and science and technology as productive forces, on the one side, and individualist ideologies and practices, on the other, is so vast that it is simply taken for granted.

In "late" capitalist societies (especially in the USA), the resulting ambiguities in economic, social, and political life, as well as in the individual and social consciousness, appear to be intractable. These ambiguities are ideologically interpreted as

[72] O'Connor, *Accumulation Crisis*.

"contingencies"; they are objectified and reified. The attitude typically adopted toward these ambiguities is ambivalency, or a kind of economic, social, and political fence-sitting. These lived ambiguities, their objectification as contingencies, and resulting ambivalent mass attitudes unintentionally help to undermine the process of valorization and accumulation. These accounts of economic and social crisis based on the individual as the "unit of analysis" are less and less satisfactory. Fits between economic, social, and political conditions and official explanations of these conditions go from bad to worse. Bad fits between social production and social needs, on the one hand, and the wage form of labor and the commodity form of need satisfaction, on the other, multiply. Ideologies and practices of individualism cease to perform their normative integration roles and become increasingly expensive materially.

Specifically, the definition of individuals in terms of property, positions, roles, files, numbers, and so on, or social integration based on the integration of living persons into ideologically defined functional roles (by contrast, system integration is based on the integration of these ideologically defined roles into one another), has two important consequences.

The first is that when living persons define themselves in terms of their relationship to abstract categories, which cease to fit actual social conditions, rather than in terms of other living persons, affect and conscience are subsumed under instrumental reason and personality integration is automatically threatened. Status attainment does not reinforce but rather undermines the individual's sense of self-worth. Ideologies of individualism which are systematically practiced with the purpose of obscuring class domination and exploitation displace social conflict into the internal personality dynamics of individuals.

At the same time, personality integration at the level of instrumental cognition depends on system integration – that is, the law of value, world market, rational state administration, political legitimation, and so on. When individuals define themselves in terms of their ideological roles, at the moment when economic disintegration, irrationalities within state crisis management, etc., destroy the "fit" between these roles, individual persons tend to lose their identities at the instrumental cognitive level. "Who am I?" cannot be answered even in terms of reified social functions; system crisis is thus experienced subjectively as personality crisis.[73]

This is one reason why it is impossible to separate the two concepts of economic-system crisis and social crisis, and why it is important to discover the ways in which they articulate with one another. Social malfunctioning is the spontaneous result of system malfunctions and vice versa. In the USA, for example, unemployment, poverty, and hard times are experienced perhaps more than anywhere else as personal failures; ideologies of individualism inevitably result in self-blame. When self-blame creates threats to the personality, the result is scapegoating, revivals of virulent racism, national chauvinism, and so on. This is inevitable in a society in which psychology treats the individual person as such (a psychology which reifies possessive, isolated, privatized individuals), rather than in terms of the totality of relationships which constitute the individual's social life. "Psychology is now a fundamental ideological tool in the construction of individual self-understanding and the support of current forms of social fragmentation."[74] It reproduces on an expanded scale the "bad fit" between individualism ideologies and real individuals, and it therefore increasingly leads to confusion (for example, the total confusion surrounding psychiatric testimony in criminal cases in the USA).

The second consequence of defining living persons in terms of ideological abstractions is that material wellbeing is defined in ideological terms of the wage and commodity forms. Social reproduction is defined not in terms of the reproduction of social relationships between living people or cooperative subjects, but rather in terms of the reproduction of ideologies

[73] This line of reasoning may illuminate why public opinion polls in the USA almost invariably conclude that the "public" has never lost faith in the economic and political systems. Rather, little faith is granted particular political leaders' desire or capacity to perform their high functions well (except when they are serving their own self-interests). What is perceived, therefore, is a crisis of social integration at the highest levels of power. System problems are thus personalized and leaders scapegoated.

[74] Richard Lichtman, letter to the author, December 1981.

and reified subjects. Given that the reproduction of capital, state, and society are defined by reference to the reproduction of ideologies of individualism and their practices, when personality crises destroy the fit between individuals and their positions and roles, system integration itself is threatened. System malfunctioning becomes the spontaneous result of social and personality crisis.

The destructive dialectic between social and system failures in this way blurs the distinction between society and economy, economy and the state, and the state and society. System and social reproduction based on ideologies and practices of individualism become permanently threatened by bad fits between living persons and economic and social functions, as well as between functions themselves. Threats to system rationality threaten social rationality, and vice versa. According to Habermas, crises do not exist until they are subjectively experienced; according to the present argument, subjective and objective crises are different aspects of the same historical process. No simple cause-and-effect relationship explains the social and psychological turmoil of the 1960s and 1970s which coexisted with inflation, unemployment, and the crisis of profitability. Rather, in the social factory, political capitalism, and administered society, social and system disintegration/ reintegration reinforce one another. The modern crisis becomes one "general crisis" which is a permanent dual threat to capital and personality and social integration. The crisis of capitalist accumulation is the crisis of the individual and society. Inflation of money and inflation of the sense of self are two elements of the same process. The counterpart of the ambiguous nature of social existence is the ambiguous economic condition called "stagflation." Individual and social crises are the crises of capital; individual crises are the way in which economic crises and crises of crisis management express themselves; economic crisis and administrative crisis are the ways in which personality crises express themselves. When the economists try to restore stability by adjusting system functions to one another, failure is preordained because the problem is not merely bad fits between system functions defined ideologically but also fits between individuals and their ideological functions. The confusion of living individuals regarding their personal and social identities is simply another aspect of the economists' and sociologists' confusion regarding economic and social modeling and economic and social policy.

Conclusion

As Marx showed, "capital" is an antagonistic social relationship within which the working class produces commodity wealth, surplus value. "Crisis" is the social and class struggle that marks the turning point in this social relationship. Since capital defined as class domination maintains itself first and foremost by individualism and other hegemonic ideologies and practices, "crisis" is social struggle within and against these ideologies and practices; the turning point with regard to their economic, social, and political efficacy; the time to decide whether to accept or reject them.

As crisis tendencies multiply, the contradictions between social production and social needs, on the one side, and individualist ideologies and practices, on the other, assume more extreme forms. In the USA of the 1980s, this form is Reaganism, an ideological neo-individualism, neo-liberalism, and neo-conservatism which adopts extreme individualistic conceptions of entrepreneurship, savings, investment, motivations, incentives, and so on, and which simultaneously attempts to contain the contradiction between social existence and individualist ideologies by restoring old identities between individualism and traditional national chauvinism, white supremacy, and patriarchal familism.[75] However, this contradiction threatens to explode at the level of popular struggles to reorganize social, economic, and political life – that is, to develop creative and self-conscious forms of cooperation within society, economy, and polity. The extreme narcissism and disconnectedness which characterize capitalism in crisis face sharper challenges from the reformed family, the local political

[75] For example, George Gilder, *Wealth and Poverty* (New York, 1981).

community, alternative forms of economic and sex/gender organization, and movements to democratize the administration of the division of social labor.

In sum, the working class and social groups today live a painful, fearful and ambiguous existence. The temptation becomes stronger to withdraw even further in order to regain individual subjectivity in tiny corners of social life not yet colonized by capital and the state administration. At the same time, the need becomes stronger to struggle to regain subjectivity through discursive reason, collective will-formation, and critical practice guided by the long war to change the wage, commodity, and other capitalist social forms within which individualism and other hegemonic ideologies and practices are produced. The fearful and partly suppressed polarization of society and its immediate political expression – Reaganism – exemplifies this tension between illusory escape into the fantasized, nostalgic, and messianic world of nineteenth-century "progress," science, and the domination of nature, on the one hand, and the struggles against racism, sexism, national chauvinism, and individualism (i.e. against reified capitalist social divisions of labor), on the other.

Class relationships and class struggles have always been structured by political, cultural, and ideological relationships, which today in crucial respects assume the form of individualism. To answer the question posed earlier – does working-class struggle include attempts to overcome divisions within itself, to establish principles of unity as a basis for collective will-formation and critical practice – the answer is yes. Needless to say, this is especially true within solidarity movements supporting Third World revolutions and class struggles.[76] It is precisely working-class struggles (defined in the broadest sense) to overcome itself "against itself" (which the transformation of the class-in-itself to a class-for-itself presupposes) and the prefigurative practices therein which constitute

[76] An example of the vast literature documenting the absence of international working-class solidarity is Don Thomason and Rodney Larson, *Where Were You, Brother? An Account of Trade Union Imperialism* (London, 1978).

the political class struggle. Only struggles which aim to unite the proletariat (broadly defined) create solid forms of social reintegration: they do so both by reconstituting "individual" to mean "social individuality and indivisibility" and by re-creating within democratic processes good fits between real people and real social, material, and political activity. Whether struggles by "quasi-groups" – for example, environmentalist and consumer groups, and ascriptive groups such as women and oppressed minorities – should be politically organized to defend themselves against charges of anarchism (hence legitimating a return to authoritarianism, which Habermas feared) remains an open question. Whether struggles within quasi-groups and ascriptive groups should obey basic principles of discursive reason and democracy as the precondition for a diversified, non-totalitarian unity definitely is not.

4

Personality Crisis

Introduction

The past two decades have yielded a wealth of theories of the crisis of the modern world. Many of these theories are based on different premises which lead to equally different conclusions – so much so that it appears that crisis theory itself is in crisis. This is and is not true. It is not true in that there is a definite theoretical and historical logic in the parade of bourgeois, neo-orthodox Marxist, and neo- and post-Marxist theories. Each comprehends reality at successively more concrete levels of human experience. Each is successively less theoretically abstract and more historically relevant.

The ancient theme of economic crisis as the result of state interference in an otherwise self-adjusting market system finds its pale reflection in modern supply-side economics. The nineteenth-century, traditional Marxist theory of capital over-production is reborn in modern neo-orthodox Marxism. The late twentieth-century theses of the "rise of subjectivity" and the displacement of economic contradictions into politics, the state, and society as a whole are mirrored in the theorums of neo-Marxism. The same may be said of the theme of capital's "spatial fix" supplied by the new international division of labor and the decentralization of productive facilities. A historical as well as theoretical coherence thus becomes visible with the aid of a critical "theory of crisis theories."

It is true that there exists a "crisis of crisis theories" in that the wealth of modern theory is made up of some coinage which is not comparable or exchangeable. The reason is the real complexity and many-sidedness of the contemporary crisis itself, together with the different theoretical and political perspectives brought to bear on the subject by a generation of crisis theorists. Worldwide there are many "joint crises"[1] – terrains of overlapping and interpenetrating economic, social, political, ideological, and personal struggles. No simple cause-and-effect or dialectical analysis of the world crisis is possible. Neither purely positivistic nor interpretive methods can illuminate fully the character of the crisis. The "whole" seems to become more mysterious. No single mind can encompass the many small and large dangers in the world today, the subtle turning points of history, the many moments of decision and testing of wills and courage. This is true, if only because in the developed capitalist world the unpredictable individual has by definition a greater role in crisis periods compared with "normal" times. Any attempt by theoreticians, therefore, to "know" the crisis in its complexity is an intellectual conceit. To experience its fullness in expressive terms, to feel the terrible uncertainty faced by masses of people, is a formula for madness. It may still be true that for most people who are privileged and trained to think about the world in critical ways the unexamined life remains worth living. But it is also true that for more than a few the fully examined life is not possible to live today.

Culture, Society, and Personality

Theoretical problems abound in the field of personality crisis as in no other. Grand theories of personality and identity have not taken us very far, although they have opened our eyes to the

---

[1] R. W. Connell, "On crisis tendencies in patriarchy and capitalism," paper delivered to the Conference of Socialist Economists, Leeds, England, July 1979. Connell defines "joint crisis tendencies" as the "coming together of crisis tendencies in a number of substructures in producing a transitional crisis of the whole; and principles ... of the joint formation of the social groups which actually become forces in the drama" (ibid., 253). Connell's focus is the analysis of sex/gender and class relations.

importance of the unconscious and the irrational. Purely Freudian objectivistic approaches to the subject have not withstood the test of time. Objectivist theories in any case have limited value because personality crisis is not only experiential in character but also has very uncertain outcomes. Subjectivistic approaches are thus essential, as Laing and others have shown. The problem arises, however, where and how to ground the experience of individual crisis cognitively and historically (a question Laing never answered). It is certainly no longer possible to infer "civilization and its discontents" from instinctual conflicts because there is no proof that a death wish and aggression instinct exist.[2] Nor is it possible to deduce personality crisis from the raw facts of economic change or hardship, unemployment, and social disorder alone.[3] The latter

[2] Even the radical Freudians can take us only so far in this field. In some works of Reich and the Marcuse of *Eros and Civilization*, there is the line that increasing pressures placed on sexuality by repressive class society must reach a limit "beyond which the biological being cannot be driven without a social crisis; or at least that the instinctual character of sexuality provides a standpoint for critique which can never be eliminated, nature thus sneaking in a kind of permanent crisis tendency" (Connell, "crisis tendencies in patriarchy and capitalism," 253). Freud's late theory of the permanent and unconscious war between the pleasure principle and aggressive death instinct provides the foundations for such views. In more benign and hopeful versions, the conflict is between the pleasure principle and socially acquired aggressive traits originating in repressive socialization, i.e. frustration of the infant by the mother-parent who trains the infant to accept the reality principle – training inevitably interpreted by the infant as repression or aggression, which then only *appears* to be instinctual. Thus what appears to be "natural" – regression in the service of the id – is learned, but "naturally learned," hence difficult but not impossible to neutralize or remove.

These universalistic theories have many variations; e.g. socialization by mothers of male youths in a male-dominated society is often cited as a source of aggression and identity crisis. "In our society . . . young males are normally brought up under the control of women; and the traumatic negation of this relation has heavy consequences in the formation of masculinity, and thence for sexual hostility in emotional life among adults" (ibid., 254).

An update of Freud's thesis of inherent instinctual conflict presented in *Totem and Taboo* is C. R. Badcock's *Madness and Modernity* (Oxford, 1983). An extreme psychoanalytic interpretation of history and civilization is Lloyd Demause's *Foundations of Psychohistory* (New York, 1982).

[3] This is the standard positivistic social science (and popular media) approach to mental disorder, suicide, crime, etc.

approach is appealing, but it is too simple, if only because individual identity cannot be casually and uncritically turned into a "dependent variable" in social theory. "Social facts" include the individual as an irreducible being. It is true that changes in "objective conditions" bear hard on identity;[4] it is equally true that personality crisis appears to occur independently of changes in "objective conditions" and may modify or alter these conditions. However, the whole theoretical problem of personality crisis and its relationship with social and economic crisis revolves around the contradiction between the self in history and history in the self – the fact that we are and are not at the same time social beings and irreducible individual bodies and minds. The theoretical issue thus becomes a problem of analyzing ambiguity. But no science yet invented permits us to infer the individual emotional effects of economic and social changes and at the same time to deduce these changes from the irreducible fact of individual internal conflict and struggle. The reason is simply that individuals *make themselves* through changes in objective conditions, which in turn depend on the particular way in which people try to resolve or escape or overcome their own personal crises.

One standard approach to this seemingly intractable issue is to explain personality and character in terms of cultural contradictions. The work of Daniel Bell is arguably the best-known example of this genre. Bell assumes the existence of a techno-economic structure which is "bureaucratic and hierarchal and a polity which believes, formally, in equality and participation." Both presuppose a personality capable of delayed gratification, responsibility, specialized roles in economic life, and a commitment to community rather than to the self first and foremost. Bell also assumes the existence of a culture of "modernity," whereby secular values have replaced religious values and the classical bourgeois character structure of "self-control and delayed gratification, of purposive behavior in the pursuit of well-defined goals" with a modernist stress on self-expression,

[4] In the interest of simplicity and tractability, I neglect the vast issue of the passage of time in the definition of personality – the relationship between personality and the past, the rites of aging, youth worship, and so on.

self-gratification, and an emphasis on the "whole" person.[5] Identity conflicts emerge from these cultural contradictions. The villain of the piece, the "seducer," is modernist culture itself, whose power derives "from the idolatry of the self."[6] According to Bell, modernist culture is a "rage against order," the "eclipse of distance" (or the attempt to achieve immediacy, impact, simultaneity, and sensation by "eliminating aesthetic and psychic distance"), and a preoccupation with artistic media which are experimented with beyond traditional aesthetic vocabularies. However, modernism proved self-exhausting; it lost its defiant rebelliousness and hence the tension which it created and which it needed to survive. In its place, there emerged a generalized disbelief, and a kind of nihilism. The crisis is therefore a "spiritual crisis, since new anchorages have proven illusory and the old ones have been submerged."[7]

Bell opts for a return to tradition and religious values to help to overcome these cultural contradictions and to resolve the modern identity crisis – a tradition which would give meaning and the continuity of the past to the present world and offer guidelines for the future, as well as ending the kind of schizo-phrenia between techno-economic work and a "swinging" life outside the workplace. This "parallel life" (in Moscivici's words) is one source of the crisis of identity, but Moscivici places the blame at the feet not of an exhausted modernity but of capitalist economic organization;[8] hence the call for changes in the nature of work itself. By contrast, Bell is certain that it is not social institutions, and certainly not capitalist production relations, which are the root of cultural disintegration and mass identity problems, but modernism itself. The search for the authentic self and the impact of experience on the self, with the moral consequences for society considered secondarily, if at all – this is the cause of the cultural and identity crisis.

[5] Daniel Bell, *The Cultural Contradictions of Capitalism* (New York, 1976), 14, xvi.

[6] Ibid., 19–20.

[7] Ibid., 28.

[8] Serge Moscivici, "The reenchantment of the world," in Norman Birnbaum (ed.), *Beyond the Crisis* (New York, 1977), 137.

Richard Sennett's and Christopher Lasch's works are loosely allied with Bell's, but take the latter's one step further. Sennett deduces the particular forms of personality crisis from a theory of culture. His premise is that personality difficulties and crises are universal, but that the way in which people experience the "warring elements" in their personalities can be explained in terms of changes in the dominant capitalist culture, specifically, the change from a Victorian personality to the modern culture of "destructive Gemeinschaft" – the expression of intimacy through other people's becoming merely mirrors of oneself and vice versa, hence the development of a "protean personality" without moral and other reference points beyond the kaleidoscopic morality of the individual self.[9] This line of argument is closely allied with Lasch's classic account of the "culture of narcissism."[10] Lasch combines a psychoanalytical and social-theoretical account. The former is based on Melanie Klein's theory that the individual's "restless, perpetually unsatisfied desire" is rooted in the absence of mature ego development (i.e. the persistence of infantile omnipotence and helplessness), which arises because of the child's inability to accept its feelings of anger toward the mother in the process of separation. Hence anger is almost invariably repressed or redirected. The social-theoretical account is based on women's demand for equality in a milieu in which men's desire for docile women remains strong; hence the "unsettling" of men by women today. Lasch argues that, in the modern personality, cognitive moral development grows beyond emotional development, and that this in turn creates the need for defense mechanisms which prevent group will-formation, i.e. which make the individual "willful," with a grandiose concept of self, fantasies of omnipotence, wealth, beauty, and so on. Lasch stresses the need for repressed anger to be expressed; although this (he adds) does not and cannot solve the problem of capitalism's illusory ideal of independence and autonomy, it can create the conditions for

[9] Richard Sennett, "Destructive Gemeinschaft," in Norman Birnbaum (ed.), *Beyond the Crisis.*

[10] Christopher Lasch, *The Culture of Narcissism: American Life in an Age of Diminishing Expectations* (New York, 1978).

personality reintegration through struggle, hence chances of group will-formation, or forms of voluntary interdependence. Otherwise, the individual's defense mechanisms doom him or her to turn moral judgments into moral inaction because action implies too much risk to identity; the ego protects itself from the consequence of cognitive development through defenses.

In Sennett's account (and by inference Lasch's), "Western man" does not define himself in terms of the meaning he has for other people but rather in terms of his power in the world and over nature. As indicated above, this means that "one has begun to conceive of that outside world as a peculiar mirror of self. It exists to fulfill the self; there are no 'human objects' or object relations with a reality all their own."[11] The effect is to banish a "sense of meaningful and *also* impersonal life which disappears."[12] In sum, one cannot see the Other's subjectivity with any objectivity, nor see one's own subjectivity in similar terms. Critical reason (as has often been said) is banished by instrumental reason and a self-serving existence. Potentially, this has frightening implications for personal identity. The belief that "one's personality is always undergoing fundamental changes, or is capable of doing so" means two things. First, because the bureaucratic and economic system promises rewards to those with ability and willingness to work hard, yet there are in fact few rewards, there occurs an epidemic of self-blame; second, when there is an intensified belief in "personality immanently disclosed in social relations," and when loving another for his or her differences, as a kind of social bonding to carry out social tasks, is replaced with a desire to find in the Other a definition of oneself, the reality of the other person is effectively erased. In a powerful passage, Sennett writes that normal conflicts in interpersonal relationships drastically change: "today people experience these unavoidable clashes as contests for personal legitimation. The appearance of an unbridgeable difference in another human being becomes a challenge to the worth of one's own self."[13] At the limit, the question arises: which person,

[11] Sennett, "Destructive Gemeinschaft," 177.
[12] Ibid., 176.
[13] Ibid., 83.

which difference, should legitimately exist at all? The roots of modern fanaticism in religion and politics are easy to find in this line of reasoning.

Peter Dreitzel expounds a more specifically (and equally pessimistic) social theory of personality, which he deduces from social crisis tendencies. "Socialization serves to produce a feeling of self-identity and group identity as well as a motivation structure within the individual on which the prevailing mode of production is psychologically based."[14] He argues that the system needs "that kind of flexible yet authoritarian social character which guarantees political apathy, instrumental rationality, and economic submission under a consumer culture." However, this is no longer possible because the family is no longer an effective agent of socialization, first, because of the increase in female-headed households and, second, because of the overflow of emotional needs not fulfilled through work. The economic and political systems' need for skilled mobile labor, with a high degree of emotional and physical control, Dreitzel continues (echoing Bell), increases the "deeply rooted emotional frustrations which lead to psychological instability of growing numbers of people."[15] The separation of economic, scientific, and technical realms from the sphere of personal life and interaction results in alienation and anomie. In work, there is a "lack of self-determination and the repression of affectivity is experienced as alienation." In the privatized sphere of one's personal relationships, symbolizations, and recreations, "the lack of guiding value standards, established modes of interpretation, and institutionalized rituals is experienced as anomie."[16]

In sum, whether it be Bell's generalized disbelief and nihilism; Lasch's narcissism, Sennett's implied fanaticism in the service of self-identity, or Dreitzel's alienation and anomie, we are presented with a powerfully pessimistic account of modern identity and identity crisis based either on cultural contradictions or on contradictions between the requirements of social

[14] Hans Peter Dreitzel, "On the political meaning of culture," in Birnbaum (ed.), *Beyond the Crisis.*
[15] Ibid.
[16] Ibid.

institutions and the individual self. The conservative as well as reformist implications of these accounts are obvious. The conservatives want a return to tradition; the reformists want a more expressive, aesthetic and communicative work and political life; revolutionary implications are conspicuous by their absence.[17]

The Meaning of Personality Crisis

We need some theoretical point of departure to speculate about the crisis of the individual and its relationship with economic and social crisis in specifically radical terms. The modern term "identity crisis" roughly resembles Plato's definition – the "hypertrophy of a human faculty . . . and the attendant atrophy of other faculties."[18] A typical example is the overdevelopment of moral cognitive powers at the expense of the emotions. In the vast literature on personality and identity, this sense of crisis as a loss of some vital power is the most common. Its premise is that the modern individual suffers from a childish helplessness/ omnipotence syndrome, which produces and is produced by feelings of deprivation and guilt, and which arises when individuals fail to couple motivations to any social will. A "willfulness' (Rollo May's term) replaces "will," which is

[17] This brief sketch of the theses of four authors is meant only to suggest the range of approaches to the problem of identity. An exhaustive treatment of the subject would take us well beyond the framework of this work and also the abilities of the author. Other highly useful works include Robert N. Bellah et al., *Habits of the Heart: Individualism and Commitment in American Life* (Berkeley, Cal., 1985); Robert W. White (ed.), *The Study of Lives* (New York, 1963); Paul Kurtz (ed.), *Moral Problems of Contemporary Society* (Buffalo, NY, 1969); Kenneth Keniston, *Youth and Dissent* (New York, 1971); Maurice Stein et al., *Identity and Anxiety* (Glencoe, Ill., 1960); Kenneth Keniston, *The Uncommitted* (New York, 1960); Robert J. Lifton, *The Life of the Self* (New York, 1976); Kai Erikson, *Everything in its Path* (New York, 1976); Grace Sevy, *The Changing Self and Capitalist Development in the United States: A Psychological and Social-Historical Analysis*, History of Consciousness Qualifying Essay, University of California, Santa Cruz, December 1977.

[18] Melvin Rader, *Marx's Interpretation of History* (New York, 1979).

something one does with others, not against others. Willfulness inevitably leads the individual to create fantasies which lead to willful acts — acts that negate reality — and which are explicable only in terms of the infantile omnipotent "I."

In William James's version, "unhealthy will" finally leads to apathy, fatigue, or exhaustion when the world does not bend to our will. The uncoupling of motivations from individual achievement, without their being recoupled to a social will, leads to anomie, apathy, helplessness. According to Melanie Klein, the willful (helpless/omnipotent) individual represses anger and pleasure, concealing them by feelings of hurt, fragility, powerlessness, fear, and helplessness at some moments, and blind optimism, hostility, and a sense of omnipotence at others. As we shall see, this dialectic between helplessness and omnipotence is universal in a society dominated by the wage form of labor and commodity form of need satisfaction: the wage and commodity forms are the main source of the modern personality crisis, which exists independently of economic, social, and political crisis tendencies.

In interpersonal relations, the helpless/omnipotent syndrome projected onto another individual provides at first a sense of relief, but more or less suddenly turns into a deeper source of distress. In this sense, crisis may be defined as the loss of power over the self and the Other with whom the self is merged or "loses itself." Romantic love, which retains its lure that the merging of personalities will produce an ecstatic power, and its ultimately destructive appeal and high status in mass culture, is the most obvious example. If I in my vulnerability alienate my power into the Other, the crisis may ensue when the Other estranges herself from me, which wounds me and makes me a stranger to myself. My investment in her turns out to be a loss for me — of me. When I seek out the Other, I am in reality seeking my lost investment, my alienated self. I have lost part of myself in her, hence I am lost without her. She is herself and part of myself at the same time. If I find her and she allows, I am something; otherwise, I am nothing — I have lost "my heart." She remains everything, "perfect and entire, wanting nothing." When I alienate myself, my self becomes an external, objective force which must be controlled at the price of psychological death. Self-control thus means control of the Other. I live with the fear of losing control of the Other, of the fear of vulnerability, of fear of fear itself. My excessive need to control rivets my attention on the Other; in my helplessness I require myself to be omnipotent. I pay no attention to myself because my self has disappeared into the Other. I have infantilized myself; I feel envious, possessive, fearful, pained, and angry – all these feelings lurk beneath one another. I feel robbed and cheated. But the Other's mere appearance (as Aristotle wisely observed) momentarily gives me back accessibility to my self.

In this account, crisis is the moment when one feels that one's identity is threatened by the loss of power over the Other into whom one has vicariously alienated one's powers. The individual undergoing crisis may rebuild a new semblance of identity on the basis of more powerful denial mechanisms. Or he may transform the self into higher levels of personality integration on the basis of coupling his motivations to a social will. The crisis moment is the turning point between the threat of isolation and fear of abandonment and the threat of loss of self and fear engulfment. The Other, deeply fearing abandonment herself, steals my self from me, which at first I carelessly toss away. The helpless Other arms herself with my self, fear of engulfment descends, and she withdraws. I may also withdraw part of my self. A crisis ensues. How much one person means to another when that person is partly or wholly ourselves – how much we permit ourselves to regress to infantile helplessness/ omnipotence – signifies the depth of modern reification. This is reflected today in the dominance of therapeutic discourse, the growing demand for intimacy and spontaneity in human relations, the growth of self-help rackets, and the mass fascination with sex, violence, and death, which have largely replaced art, science, and politics as the most popular subjects of our age.

In sum, crisis revolves around the theme of the felt or perceived loss of power or threats to our power which we have alienated into the Other (just as labor alienates its power into capital). Just as capital falsely disempowers labor and falsely empowers itself, individuals induced by commercial culture falsely disempower themselves in personal relations, in this way falsely empowering the Other. Individuals become ripe for emotional exploitation (just as alienated labor is ripe for economic exploitation). We produce a surplus personal value, i.e. a kind of power in the Other in whom we alienate ourselves (just as labor produces a surplus value for capital). The Other seeks to "realize" this "surplus value" and power and accumulate more power (just as capital seeks to realize surplus value in the market to accumulate more alienated labor). He who has alienated his power, who feels falsely powerless in relation to her, she with a surplus of personal value, who feels falsely powerful in relation to him, faces two kinds of identity crisis: the former characterized by feelings of deprivation and fears of abandonment, the latter by feelings of guilt and fears of engulfment. With a "normal neurosis," the self and the Other pull part-way back; in place of a full fusion of personalities, there is a kind of shading of two selves into one another; mutual fears of abandonment and engulfment are muted; romance is understood to be a false path to identity. Internal conflicts between feelings of being nothing and feelings of being everything achieve a kind of unstable equilibrium. Here is perhaps the meaning of the achievement of Freud's "general level of unhappiness."

Crisis presupposes some event which threatens loss or engulfment, and which either is or appears to be external to individuals. This event, such as loss of power over the Other, activates or reactivates internal conflicts or the "warring elements of their personalities."[19] These warring elements originate in infancy and childhood, probably at the unknown moment when the child becomes conscious that he or she is a separate person. More or less painful experiences inevitably follow. The warring elements (internal conflicts) create unconscious compulsions to re-create and relive early painful experiences with the blind purpose of "making them come out all right," for example, to win the love of a parent surrogate into whom one projects one's ego ideal, hence about whom one has deeply conflicted feelings. External events which activate inter-

---

[19] Sennett, "Destructive Gemeinschaft," 171. This expression, not the theory presented here, except when explicitly noted, is Sennett's.

nal conflicts thus may themselves be created by the projection of unconscious conflicts. When an individual projects conflicted feelings into present relationships, compulsive self-destructive and destructive actions are usually not very far behind. These actions may presuppose changes in "objective conditions," such as unemployment, or business failure, or divorce made possible by the material independence of women. But self-destructiveness and destructiveness in their subtle and crude forms, including social violence, can and do occur independently of changes in objective conditions, and may modify these conditions.

It is theoretically possible to deduce the effects of system disintegration on the stability of social life and personality or identity. It is also in principle theoretically possible to deduce the effects of personality crisis on social and system integration. Not only is society in the self; the self is also in society. Causal arrows between self and society run both ways. Institutionalized divorce has an impact on social solidarity and material life, just as farm bankruptcies affect the self-esteem of farmers. The death of a loved one, separation and divorce, loss of a valued job – any abrupt change which threatens a person's denial mechanisms, hence self-identity and emotional security – have social and economic effects. So do abrupt internal changes which appear and reappear in seemingly unpredictable ways and which activate the "warring elements" in ourselves. Traumas evolve; psychological conditions yesterday affect not only psychological but also social and economic conditions today – in perhaps fateful and unknowable ways.

Internal conflict breaks out along three related dimensions of experience. One is the level of animal sensation. Another is the level of pre-verbal images. A third is the level of cognition – opinions, judgments, conclusions. The first level is physiological. Internal conflict is felt as raw anger versus fear; fear versus psychological pain; fear and pain (anxiety) versus anger; and other combinations of basic sensations which we share with other mammals. Conflicted feelings may be moderate, or so extreme and threatening that the individual subdues them by some form of psychic numbness or depression (or absence of feelings) which may be experienced as a great relief, however much psychological theory interprets depression as a psychic problem.

The second level is pre-verbal imagery. In an identity crisis, individuals typically have conflicted mental pictures of the parent, sibling, boss, or the Other which are more or less extreme positive and negative idealizations.[20] These images erupt from the barely conscious mind into consciousness, and appear as obsessions which are often acted out in compulsive ways with definite social and economic as well as emotional effects.

The third level is cognitive. "Warring elements" consist of conflicted premises and judgments and evaluations of the Other. These thoughts are also typically positive and negative idealizations fighting one another.

Different people in different circumstances structure conflicted sensations, images, and thoughts in different ways. I may feel angry with my fear; be frightened by my anger; feel fear when I anticipate pain or threats to pleasure; feel angry when I entertain a particular image of the Other; feel relief at the thought of inflicting pain on the Other; judge the Other according to positive and negative idealizations which jump into my conscious mind when I feel anxious, and so on. Intensive and informed self-observation may untangle these feelings, mind pictures, and thoughts – a self-observation which itself is a painful experience and which at the limit risks madness.

"Knowledge" of personality crisis thus requires highly disciplined scientific analytical abilities and creative interpretive skills. A "good" analyst has discovered some method for answering the question: "When do I deploy my analytical powers and when do I bring into play my intuitive and interpretive abilities?" In any relationship burdened by mechanisms of trans-

---

[20] In the huge literature on the subject, I have found Theodor Reik's *Of Love and Lust: On the Psychoanalysis of Romantic and Sexual Emotions* (New York, 1967) most helpful. It might be added that behaviorists use our proclivity for negative and positive idealization to "help" patients overcome separation anxiety by methods which reinforce negative images while banishing positive ones.

ference and counter-transference (that is, any significant emotional relationship), therapists can make big mistakes quite unwittingly and can achieve big successes without any "reasonable" explanation why they have occurred – which is a truism in the mental health professions. In sum, however complex are these warring elements, whatever individual variations are present, whoever suffers from a self which is an emotional battleground, whatever the nature of the therapy – personality crisis doubtless not only affects the mental health of individuals undergoing crisis but also has the implications for social motivations, economic performance, and political beliefs.

Inner conflicts which trigger instinctual and quasi-instinctual distressful feelings (e.g. anger and aggression, respectively) will be expressed in different culturally and ideologically determined forms in different modes of production (and in different phases in the development of any particular mode of production). The fetishistic and reified character of capitalist existence screens and sorts and censors experience and memory in ways that create historically specific forms and manifestations of inner conflicts.[21] The words we use to describe our feelings are also socially and historically determined. For example, I may say that I "feel guilty" when I am not working and "feel deprived" when I have to work, when actually I am *thinking* that I am guilty and deprived, and *feeling* one of two forms of anxiety: fear layered on psychic pain, and pain layered on fear, respectively. These kinds of distorted self-expression flow from the cultural dominance of "mind" and the marginalization of "body" and "feeling" in Western capitalism. The only way to overcome distorted self-expression is to develop a physiological awareness of the four sensations registered by our animal brain in the same way that the brain of other mammals registers raw feelings – these being pleasure, pain, fear, and anger.

Relived or renewed emotional trauma activates not only warring elements in the individual's personality but also a

[21] The classic account of the social and ideological unconscious mind in modern capitalism is Richard Lichtman, *The Production of Desire: The Integration of Psychoanalysis into Marxist Theory* (New York, 1982).

process whereby he or she who suffers attempts to relieve the suffering. Well-known techniques – repression, sublimation, and projection – are rebuilt or redeployed by the unconscious mind to reduce levels of distress or anxiety. However, it is inevitable that repressed feelings "leak out sideways" in definite ways.[22] For example, repressed anger may "leak out" as hostility or passive aggression, or take on physical forms. Repressed fear and pain may leak out as "hurt and helpless" feelings. It is also inevitable that projected feelings re-create or reconstruct morbid forms of a sense of false power and false powerlessness – a kind of universal manic-depression syndrome. And that conflicted feelings sublimated into work or creative activity result in work products which may show signs of these conflicts. The repression, sublimation, and projection of feelings may lead the individual away from, not toward, the "general level of unhappiness."

The precise moment of personality crisis is the turning point at which repression, sublimation, and projection mechanisms begin to crumble and the conflicts become apparent – the dangers and opportunities that await when defenses and denial mechanisms begin to fail; the threatened loss of power when what one is able to take for granted in relation to the Other is thrown into doubt; the sudden transformation from fears and pains of engulfment to those of abandonment and vice versa. This crisis moment – the transition between manic depression or omnipotence/helplessness – triggers an internal struggle which assumes as many forms as there are possibilities for human self-expression. Normally, the individual attempts more or less desperately to reconcile conflicted feelings, images, and thoughts which in the crisis can no longer be muted by defense and denial mechanisms. The attempt to reconcile the irreconcilable makes things worse; therapy itself becomes a kind of self-induced suffering. In Sennett's words,

it is a psychological truism that people experience crises which reinforce the warring elements in their personalities, rather than break

---

[22] I learned this expression from Georgia Rynick of the Twin Tiers Resource Center in Binghamton, NY.

up these elements or give one side a victory over the other. Every therapist will have spent hours with clients who are in the grip of emotions which cannot be reconciled. This is a struggle in which the force of emotion acquires a more powerful hold over the client, the longer he or she attempts a reconciliation.[23]

However, if the vulnerable individual is armed with social and psychological insights (the only weapon at his or her disposal) about the self in society and society in the self, there is the possibility of a redefinition of crisis as "transformation," or higher levels of personality integration which presuppose a commitment to struggle personally and politically against the reified and fetishistic existence of the wage and commodity forms.

In this event, crisis resolution does not presuppose the rebuilding of stronger defense systems and denial mechanisms but rather a sense of humility in the face of the powerful socially reified unconscious and a sense of confidence born of the reconceptualization of self as a more social individual. This transformation brings a kind of pleasure, with new empathetic powers which permit a more objective understanding of our own subjectivity and that of others. For example, personality crisis derives in part from social isolation, which makes individuals vulnerable to power-tripping by others. In this way, we begin to define outselves less in terms of the "protean self" and more in terms of our self in society, and society in our self. Our ego ideal becomes more social and less individual; we can become moral historical subjects. Our tolerance for ambiguity increases. Our personal emancipation cannot be complete without social emancipation from a reified existence; social emancipation is impossible without a measure of personal freedom. Our sense of personal and of social morality becomes more inseparable in practice; principles of individual and social morality have real underpinnings, no longer based solely on nostalgia for real or imagined lost traditions. We are thus able to redefine ourselves less in terms of the instrumental meaning

---

[23] Sennett, "Destructive Gemeinschaft."

that others have for ourself; and more in terms of the emotional and political meaning we have for others.

Precisely because personality crisis poses dangers and opportunities and is a time of intense inner struggle, it is also a time for decision; a testing of wills and courage. Moral choices must be made. If the crisis strikes as a threat of the loss of control over self and the Other, the line of least resistance is the reconstruction of denial mechanisms, or the illusion of the recapture of self-power and power over the Other. This is the ever-present danger facing those undergoing personality crisis. The opportunity, the line of maximum advantage, is the chance to gain a social power with others. Crisis defined as the restructuring of the defensive personality is the rebuilding of powers of taking care of and being taken care of by others, or infantilization and self-infantilization of others. Crisis as transformation is the development of new social powers of taking care with others. In sum, transformation is a conjuncture in the development of personality in which the individual can no longer attempt to reconcile internal conflicts, because they are so extreme that they can no longer be held in check; it is a moment when the individual yields to one of the conflicted feelings and thus marginalizes the other – "to give one side a victory," in Sennett's words. The individual undergoing crisis faces not only a personal but also a political choice.

Modern Capitalism and Personality Crisis

Cultural and biological theories of identity crisis (discussed in the second section of this chapter) are ideological. They are backward-looking and naturalistic, respectively. They ignore the question, what is a specifically capitalist personality crisis in the epoch of the universalization of the wage and commodity form – of permanent revolution and counter-revolution? Cultural and biological theories may explain distress and depression, anxiety and anomie, not crisis defined in terms of inner struggle and possibilities of personal and political transcendence, or the reintegration of the self along social-political as well as "derepressive" lines. We need to speculate about personality crisis in ways that are faithful to the meaning of "crisis" as a struggle for power and emancipation.

We know that capital is rushing madly through the present; it has raced headlong into a crisis. It attempts to reduce its turnover time compulsively and obsessively. Modernization of production, internationalization of production, and a bloated debt structure are three sides of a single process. Whole communities and cities are thrown away in the rush to defend and expland profits. "Growth coalitions" multiply like cancer cells, killing the normal cells of family, religion, tradition. The frenzy of accumulation; the fear that it will come to an end in a huge crash or environmental or military catastrophe; the unbelievable excesses of late capitalism worldwide – these bear witness to the obsessive–compulsive quality of the inner soul of capital. If we could become its inner eye, if we could transport ourselves into its inner soul, if we could hear the relentless beat of accumulation, we could experience as well as know the madness of this obsessiveness – this world where capital and money are a religious and aesthetic experience, and where power is a moral category. When we examine ourselves, we find capital within our own souls. We too rush through the present; we race for some victory – or toward some unknown destination; we are governed by unlimited desire; we stumble and fall from identity into the abyss. We create our own personal crisis, as capital creates its own crisis.

At a certain level of meaning, economic and social crisis and personality crisis are indistinguishable. In the crisis, capital is obsessed with regaining control over labor; we are obsessed with regaining control over the Other, a thing, our objectified self, not ourselves defined as our relationships. When we objectify ourselves – when we make ourselves external and foreign to ourselves – we are compelled to regain control and regulate the Other, just as capital is required to regulate labor. The objective breakdown in the circuits of capital and the subjective breakdown in the "circuits" of everyday social life are nothing more nor less than the breakdown of the self and its alienation in the Other. At some unknown point in this process, capital can no longer regulate itself, the state cannot regulate capital, and the individual can no longer regulate him/herself.

Capital's passion, money in search of more of itself, is unregulated by public conscience, institutionalized morality, or the state. The individual is bereft of a trustworthy social superego; neither capital nor the state can administer the passions and conscience. The individual is thus isolated, not merely materially and socially, but emotionally, a "stranger in the crowd." In a reified world, a world of illusion, when capital, state, and love itself are self-negating because real love threatens the Other's mask, how can the individual express instinctual impulses in traditional disguised forms, yet in ways that lead to meaningful actions – when the disguised forms of the instincts are themselves disguised?

In this cauldron of uncertainty and insecurity, a world where most people are encouraged to aspire to the banal, the routine, the scheduled, personality crisis erupts. In an epoch of the domination of the wage and commodity forms, in a culture that worships individualism, the individual is deprived of real supports for the exaggerated demands of the personality.

Does the wage form reproduce infantile fears of engulfment, while ameliorating fears of abandonment? And does the commodity form of desire reproduce infantile fears of abandonment, while ameliorating fears of engulfment? And do both function as basic social defenses against the void, nothingness, against loss of identity or the fear of psychic death? The wage form provides the structured existence which functions as the parent surrogate; its discipline places limits on the individual's expression and behavior; it unites people into a common, albeit alienated and exploitative, bond without which sanity is impossible. It is the universal "no," and at worst it is an act of aggression.

The commodity form of desire gives free rein to the flighty, unpredictable, possessive self; it provides rich opportunities to "act out." It is the grounds for exploration, inventiveness, and experimentation – not through the individual's direct social relationships, but rather through the individual's relation to self-possessed objects and things. Commodity desire is the child's desire for its toy as a personality prop – the child who does not know and cannot know what meaning its own life has for the Other.

Capitalism is a kind of family in which individuals live highly structured yet precarious. existences within the wage form, existences broken by daily periods of acting out within the commodity form. Self-expanding capital requires individuals to want "more" – more regression in the service of the id; hence more inner chaos; hence more need for the structured existence of the wage form. Capital is forced to be universal parent (hence the current fad of "corporate culture"). Capitalist accumulation, once built on solid social-psychological foundations, destroyed these foundations. Historically, capital accumulated through economic and social crises; today capital accumulates through personality crises as well. The crisis-ridden personality becomes the material which capital uses and adapts to restructure itself. It channels the fear and anger that it has produced into new forms of discipline, patriotism, self-blame. Or it abandons what it regards as its hopeless children clinging to worn-out institutions such as trade unions and the welfare state, for greener pastures in the Third World. Is it possible that the limit of capital is capital itself, defined in terms of the character structures which it produces? Certainly, the individual has nowhere to escape to; identification with ascriptive and quasi-ascriptive groups tends to be uncritical and routinized. Identification with economic class is tenuous. New social movements are half blind to everything except their own narrow desires – blind even to the ways in which they place stresses and strains on economic, social, and political systems. And the leaders of the organized labor movement long ago suppressed even the concept of working class.

More specifically, individuality based on autonomous control of productive forces has been replaced by complex ideologies of individualism. Psychologically, the individual ego has become weaker, even as the illusion of the strong ego in Hollywood and television becomes more widespread. As Foucalt has shown, the ego is not only weak but decentered; it is difficult to speak of a central individual human subject. As Russell Jacoby said, "There is talk of identity and identity crisis, security and insecurity, authenticity and bad faith, not because there is a viable ego faced with too many options, but because there is no ego faced with no options." This weak, fragmented ego underlies the modern identity crisis. We are supposed to be strong individually; we have in fact rather weak ego identities.

Meanwhile, the goal of "self-realization" means that impulse controls become unhinged. The lid is ripped off the id. Libinal energy itself becomes commodified, reified in pop music videos. There lurks the ever-present danger of mass regression to aggressive states in the service of the id. Drugs become normalized as medicine for the personality in distress. At the same time, as culture critics stress, the superego and ego ideals are less and less formed by internalized parental athority. Ego ideals become elusive. They are subject more and more to the whims of the immediate group. Individual morality based on definite social principles, whether or not these principles are enshrined in law and religion, has largely disappeared. In the absence of a public language of conscience, morality becomes transformed into something one negotiates with oneself in the context of particular situations which confer advantages and threaten penalties. Criminals are sorry for getting caught, not for committing a crime. Individuals are sorry when their betrayals and disloyalties are exposed and cover-ups break down, not for committing these emotional crimes. It is considered natural for the individual to use others for his or her own ambition; Kantian ethics, based historically on the tension between use- and exchange-value in the epoch of small commodity production, disappear.

The internal struggle is therefore the struggle of the weak ego to regulate the demands of the desirous and socially encouraged power-seeking id, on the one hand, and the demands of a protean group morality, on the other. It is not only a question of the "protean individual" who can be anything or do anything; it is also a question of the "protean group" which can decree peace and justice one day and practice jingoism and racism the next. No individual solution to this internal struggle can be found, not for the individual who stands between unknown and unlimited desire and unknown and uncertain rules of conduct. No strong patriarchal superego can be appropriated and deployed to solve the problem; religious fundamentalism only appears to wipe out guilt from past sins; unquestioning patriotism works only when awesome military forces invade and inhabit the corpse of revolutions (e.g. Grenada). Yet patriarchy itself is far from dead, despite the hammer blows by feminism; it can return with a vengeance; a religion that promises to save souls instantly has made its revival; regressive nationalism also has returned.

This is why we can speak of a "crisis": no one knows or can know the future of struggles of labor, new social movements, and individual men and women, nor the power of reaction by the forces of unreason. This is the central issue, because conscience and morality are required to be grounded in reason. But the democratization of Romantic expressionism through consumerism has been associated with a loss of the intelligibility and hope promised by the age of reason. To be expressive in the age of unreason risks a form of madness; expressivity today is grounded not in hope and intelligibility, but in irrationality and cognitive dissonance. Repressed affect thus becomes universal. Hostility, hurt-and-helplessness, manic pleasures, projection, sublimation – all defense mechanisms work overtime. They must work as fast as the pace of modern life itself. Values and norms are nonexistent in an amoral society without shame or even guilt. No moral grounding for political consent exists. Nor is there any philosophy of hope which can cognitively ground affectivity. If there is nothing in which to ground morality, there is no measure which the ego can employ to regulate id desire. The id thus rules; the weak ego cannot possibly regulate libidinal desire in all its forms; sex and power merge into the "seductive society" with its endless personal manipulations and open brutalities in the form of mass rape and killing. Can we not provisionally conclude that only a collective ego and a collective reason and a collective morality can possibly govern the modern hyperactive id?

In the context of vast and unknowable economic and social changes which threaten not only the substance but also the forms of Western democratic traditions, the individual is bewildered and anxious, caught between the demands of the "apparatus" (the institutionalized and opportunistic state morality) and the provincial claims of the "territory," where inward-lookingness is the norm, where wholeheartedness to insiders and meanspiritedness to outsiders and newcomers are not so uncommon. How can the weak ego regulate the relationship between instinctual and quasi-instinctual impulses (especially when these impulses themselves are in conflict with one another) and the demands of the apparatus and territory or both? No one is capable of such an emotionally heroic task. Every possible self-doubt is triggered; every attempt to find oneself brings more misery. Escapism leads to more morbid symptoms, idle illusions of independence. Is it any wonder that the problem of authority and social integration has returned as a central topic of discussion?

Is there a resolution to the personality crisis today? And, if so, what is it? We can only speculate. Personality crisis means a turning point in personality development; a time for decisions about life choices and actions; a struggle with the regressed id and the shifting yet compulsive morality of the reference group. Crisis occurs in that instant when defense and denial mechanisms fail; when the mask is torn away; when the wall that separates the individual from the Other begins to crumble; when vulnerability threatens the false sense of self-identity based on ideologies of individualism. This moment poses the danger of helplessness, a false sense of powerlessness. The "crisis" is thus the moment when there is at least a slim possibility of the individual freeing himself or herself from routine, destructive, and at the limit murderous and suicidal games; the moment when the individual begins to be unmasked yet holds the mask half protecting his face (as it were); the moment when the individual begins to feel vulnerable, but before this vulnerability degenerates into a sense of helplessness and hopelessness, cynicism or despair. Each second today brings countless moments such as these, most of them passing obsessively and routinely from the manic to the depressive, only to pass back again when defenses are rebuilt and strengthened, when the individual learns to become more cagey, alert to danger, manipulative, less ethical.

This moment of crisis is precisely when transformation into a social individuality becomes theoretically possible. But one must catch oneself at the turning point and glimpse the Other as neither the powerless child nor the all-powerful embodiment of the ego ideal, but rather as another crisis victim. At this moment, one can externalize the internal struggle, or know and feel that the ways in which one suffers are also the ways in which others suffer, grasp suffering as a social process, externalizing suffering through social and political struggle. We have examples, however limited and in their own way distorted.

Alcoholics Anonymous seizes the crisis moment and at best transforms it into a newfound sense of humility and self-confidence, although AA relies on a spiritual *deus ex machina*. Political meetings at their rare best can have the same effect – of instilling a sense of patience and irony, a sense of "commit and see." So can group therapy sessions, however isolated and unreal these are in terms of the dominant economic, social, and political questions of the day. These momentary transfigurations or metamorphoses, which always contain the seeds of retreat and regression, are characterized by two basic facts. The first is that, during crisis and transformation, truth can be found nowhere in practice; truth lies in consciousness and cognition and is accessible only to theory. The awkward and painful personal struggles; the yielding to the imperatives of the social struggle; the humility before a world trying to emancipate itself in the most dangerous and harsh conditions; the confidence that one's efforts count for something – in this setting, new situations and experiences are created which are incomprehensible in terms of the hegemonic language, the discourse of individualism, that we use day to day in matter-of-fact ways.

The experience of crisis and transformation demands a new language, new interpretive methods, new disassociations and reassociations, which is the province of theory, not common sense. The *second* truth is that "theory," defined in this sense and used at this level of experience, means something so simple that it is often overlooked. It is based on the Greek tradition and rejects out of hand the Christian tradition of original sin. It presupposes that knowledge, truth, and goodness are inseparable.

Theory is no more nor less than the critique of the self-deceptions which we use to legitimate to ourselves the deceptions of others. This means simply that we cannot know why we are deceived or why we deceive others until we first know why others deceive themselves and why we deceive ourselves. No trust, hence no morality, is possible without knowledge of our own and others' self-deceptions. Without trust, hope has no ground, and without hope, the last thing we give up in life, it is inevitable that the crisis at all levels will be resolved by more oppressive structures of domination including self-domination. In this case, our children and grandchildren will have to start all over again. Do we wish that burden on them?

Index

Index by Meg Davies